ReB FLEKAER

UNDERSTANDING
PERSONAL AND BUSINESS
FINANCE

Understanding Personal and Business Finance

W. Reay Tolfree

WOODHEAD-FAULKNER · CAMBRIDGE

Published by Woodhead-Faulkner Ltd
8 Market Passage, Cambridge CB2 3PF

First published 1981
© W. Reay Tolfree 1981
ISBN 0 85941 150 8

Photoset by Watkiss Studios Ltd
Biggleswade, Bedfordshire
Printed in Great Britain by
Butler & Tanner Ltd, Frome and London

Contents

Contents

About this book

People are nowadays taking a great deal of interest in the details of the money aspects of their own daily lives. They are not only becoming more conscious of the substantial deductions made from their gross pay, but they are also checking on such things as the relative costs of hire purchase, budget accounts, bank loans, credit cards and insurance policies, and on the income yields they might be getting from different kinds of investment. People are much more sophisticated, money-wise, than they used to be, and are asking themselves many questions about personal finance that those of an earlier generation couldn't be bothered about.

This book seeks to provide for such enquiring minds a broad outline of factual knowledge of the financial world so far as it affects the average man or woman in his or her daily affairs. The contents of the book have been specially selected and arranged so that they also provide a complete course of study for candidates for the new GCE Ordinary (Alternative) Level subject of *Personal and Business Finance*. The syllabus for this subject, as one would expect, covers very much the same ground as that which the alert and numerate citizen is seeking to explore for his own satisfaction and personal benefit.

It is impossible in any practical book on money matters to avoid using figures. Unfortunately, in times of rapid inflation any mention of prices, wage levels, interest rates and taxes rapidly becomes out of date. Figures used in this book were realistic in the autumn of 1980, but allowance must be made by the reader for changes in economic conditions since then. Although absolute figures may become dated the principles concerned, and in particular the relationships between different figures, stay more or less unchanged.

A selection of additional reading and of material available for the help of teachers is listed at the end of the book.

Acknowledgements

The author wishes to acknowledge with deep appreciation his indebtedness to the large number of people whose help and criticism have contributed to this book. Not only have they provided information and expertise but in some cases have read preliminary drafts of complete chapters and offered helpful comments. Any errors that remain, however, are the author's own.

In particular his thanks are tendered to the following:

Alan Sugden, for his help with Chapters 6, 13 and 14;

Lloyds Bank, for permission to reproduce some of the present author's material originally published in the bank's 'Money matters' feature in the *UK Press Gazette;*

Lloyds Bank's Pay Service and Investment, Taxation and Economics Departments;

The Building Societies Association;

Lloyds & Scottish Finance Ltd;

The Company Pensions Information Service;

The College of Insurance;

The British Insurance Brokers' Association.

PART ONE

Personal income

1 Wages and salaries

Most people earn their living by working for somebody else – for a small firm, a company or a public authority. In other words, they sell their effort, whether on the factory floor or in an office, hospital, school or wherever, to other people who are able to use it for producing goods or services that have value to the community and can be either sold to willing purchasers or paid for by the public through taxation.

The majority of individuals, therefore, are employees working for a wage or salary. And, although it may be true that the payment we receive for working is not our sole purpose in working, it is a very important factor, possibly the most important, in our working lives. So let us first look at rates of pay and at the various bases on which such rates may be assessed.

Time rates

The most commonly understood basis for remuneration is the time rate. The employer agrees to pay and the worker to accept a stated amount of money for a specified period of work. The period selected can be an hour, day, week, month or year, according to the nature and regularity of the work and the status of the employee. An office worker, for instance, will usually work for an agreed sum per year, called a salary. He or she will draw one-twelfth of this sum each calendar month, irrespective of the number of days in the month. Although there may be a requirement regarding minimum hours to be worked in a given period, the main criterion for measuring the work performed by a salary earner is not the number of hours put in, but the adequacy of the performance of the job for which he or she has been appointed. At the other extreme, a home help or jobbing gardener will often be paid at so much per hour worked.

The most usual example of a time rate is the fixed wage per week of a standard number of hours – say 37½ hours consisting of five days each of 7½ hours. The employee has to attend for work at the stated times and perform the required duties. The actual amount of work he in fact performs does not affect his pay, although were he to shirk, or were the supply of work to dry up altogether, he might find himself laid off, provided the terms of his employment permitted this.

Because there is no measured check on the amount of work performed it is common for workers on pure time rates to be appropriately supervised. In the case of salaried administrative or executive personnel, supervision takes the form of the employee being responsible directly to his superior. In the case of a large number of shop-floor workers a system of clocking on and off ensures that the required number of hours worked is correct, and the employing of a foreman or overseer ensures that workers are not idle and that their output is up to standard in quality and quantity.

Depending on the terms of employment there may be penalties for absence. Commonly, any period of non-attendance short of the standard day or week will involve a deduction in pay at the hourly rate. For example, if the standard week is 38 hours and the standard wage £76 per week, a shortage of one hour or a part of an hour during the week could result in a deduction of one hour at the equivalent hourly rate (in this case £2) from the week's wage. There may, of course, be provision for penalties to be calculated on a different formula.

Where an employee is required to attend eight hours a day (as distinguished from 40 hours per week) he might even suffer a deduction for lateness one morning even though he were to make up the lost time on another day. It is important to discover the *exact* terms of employment before accepting a job.

Overtime

Where the volume of work to be done exceeds what can be completed in the normal working day, extra hours worked are usually paid at higher than standard rates, often at half as much again. Work required at weekends or on public holidays usually attracts double pay. It is customary, for convenience in making out time sheets and wage slips, for the higher hourly pay for overtime work to be expressed in terms of time instead of cash. Thus two

3

hours' overtime at 150% of the basic wage rate would be expressed as three hours' extra work. It comes to the same thing, of course, but this practice does explain why overtime is often said to be paid at 'time and a half' instead of 'wage and a half'.

Overtime work may be optional, compulsory or guaranteed. If it is optional you may decline to work overtime if you choose. If your contract of employment obliges you to work overtime when called upon to do so with reasonable notice you do not have a choice; were you to decline you would doubtless suffer some penalty such as loss of bonus. In some occupations, notably in those industries that are overmanned or in which trade unions have succeeded in shortening the standard working week, your employment contract might guarantee you the availability of overtime. In a very few industries overtime is both guaranteed and compulsory.

Example

(*a*)   Basic wage for a standard 38-hour week is £76. Overtime is paid at time and a half. Ten hours' overtime a week is guaranteed to be available. Five hours' overtime is compulsory.

(*b*)   Basic wage for a standard week of 42 hours is £84. Overtime is paid at time and a half. Eight hours' overtime a week is guaranteed, of which three hours are compulsory.

A person is willing to work 45 hours per week. Which employer will pay him the larger weekly wage?

Answer   (*a*)   £76 + (7 × £3) = £97
                (*b*)   £84 + (3 × £3) = £93

So (*a*) will pay more.

In certain large organisations overtime rates are calculated on a rising scale, *e.g.* first hour per week at standard hourly rate, second hour at time and a quarter, remainder at time and a half. Overtime in clerical and administrative occupations is uncommon.

Advantages of time rates

Time rates are the most widespread basis for renumeration, although they are often subject to modification by the application of certain features of work measurement technique (*see* page 6). The main circumstances in which pure time rates are appropriate are:

(*a*)   where output cannot be measured (*e.g.* a local government officer);

(*b*)   where rate of output is determined not by the individual but by the speed of a machine or process (*e.g.* operator of a canning machine);

(*c*)   where quality of work or time taken per unit of output is not the primary essential (*e.g.* a door-keeper);

(*d*)   where output is largely irrelevant (*e.g.* that of a trainee or learner);

(*e*)   where safety and caution take priority over output (*e.g.* drivers of public service vehicles).

Pure time rates are broadly appropriate for the unskilled and the very highly skilled, and also for clerical, administrative and policymaking employees.

Disadvantages of time rates

The disadvantages of time rates include:

(*a*)   lack of inbuilt incentive for efficient and rapid work;

(*b*)   need for continuous supervision on the shop floor, necessitating grading of workers according to their efficiency (*e.g.* improvers, rank-and-file workers, team leaders, shift leaders, foremen);

(*c*)   possible resentment arising from wage differentials between the various grades.

Motivation

Two main methods adopted for providing motivation for shop-floor time workers are as follows.

1.   Allotting a given quantity of work per shift, and allowing the members of the shift to leave when the quota has been completed, payment being made for the standard shift. This is possible only where tasks are readily definable. The system does encourage hasty and slipshod work.

2.   Modifying the pure time rate by applying some degree of work measurement. Thus, for example, output targets can be set, with bonuses payable for exceeding the target. Bonuses may take the form of a higher hourly rate for time worked *after* target completion, or of a specific payment per unit of output exceeding the target.

Piece rates

The simplest form of piece rate to understand is that of the early nineteenth-century home worker in a cottage industry. The worker was provided with a measured quantity of material, was loaned the necessary tools, and was paid a fixed sum for each unit of output. This system is still used for remunerating part-time addressers of envelopes and other home operators doing routine work.

It is widely recognised that time worked is not an adequate measure of the work done, since it takes no account of efficiency, skill, effort and speed. This can be partly but not wholly offset by a more or less complicated system of gradings and differentials, and by job evaluation.

The adoption of pure piece rates – pay according to size of output – is an attempt to overcome this, but in its raw form it becomes a source of friction between workers. For example, where a brick-layer is paid per 100 bricks laid, some workers could draw twice the wage of others for the same time spent working. It is nevertheless true that where output per worker can be easily measured, and the quality is of a readily recognised standard, piece work can be a powerful incentive to increased production.

Advantages of piece rates

Source of the main advantages of piece rates are as follows.

1. The employee has a major incentive to increase his production. Under pure time rates any benefits from higher production accrue only to the employer; under modified piece rates benefits are shared by employer and employee.
2. Setting targets for output provides a form of job satisfaction, especially where the task, being essentially repetitive, does not itself provide any sense of achievement.
3. The potentially high earnings attract efficient workers.
4. There is less need for supervision, although quality control becomes more important.
5. The individual has more scope for pride in his work.

Disadvantages of piece rates

There are certain disadvantages of piece rates. They include the following.

1. Complicated systems of calculation are hard for the worker to understand.
2. Earnings, although generally higher, can be less stable, predictable or secure.
3. The guaranteed basic pay is usually lower than it would be under pure time rates.

In practice it is often found that a combination of time work and piece work gives the best results in terms both of increased productivity and of labour relations.

Example

Standard output of average operator is 15 units per hour. For a standard week of 39 hours the guaranteed basic wage is £70.20. This factory operates a so-called 'time allowed' rate system of bonuses. This means that it pays piece rates calculated at the time allowed for the standard output for any excess of output produced by an operator.

A given operator produces 825 units in a particular week. What will be his gross pay?

Answer   15 units per hour for 39 hours = 585 units, which is therefore the standard weekly output per man.
Standard weekly wage is £70.20.
Therefore 'time allowed' rate is 12p.
Gross pay is 825 × 12p = £99.

Commission

Individuals employed in many branches of the marketing or selling function of an industry are frequently paid a fixed salary (time work) plus commission on sales (piece work). The commission is usually expressed as a percentage of the value of sales over a period. It may be payable on total sales at a relatively low percentage, or only on sales exceeding agreed target figures, in which case it would be at a higher rate.

In some occupations, notably that of insurance salesmen, there is often no salary at all, all remuneration being by way of commission.

Conditions of work

A form of incentive more widely adopted today than in former years is that of profit sharing. This is the sharing of a predetermined portion of the annual company profits with each member of the work force, usually in proportion to his or her wage or salary. This is too indirect for it to be an important productivity incentive since the size of the company profits is quite outside the control of any individual employee.

The main purpose of profit sharing is to bring a feeling of belonging, of participation in the activity of the company, to each employee. Nevertheless, it may still form part of total remuneration and is not a feature to neglect in assessing the total reward to be derived from any given employment.

The earning of wages, salaries, bonuses, commission and profit sharing – the sum of the cash remuneration – is not the only purpose most of us have in taking employment. Indeed, we might actually enjoy the work we do for its own sake! Unless we have been brought up to a life of complete leisure, most of us obtain a greater or lesser degree of personal satisfaction and fulfilment from earning our living. We have only to notice that we are much less bored when we are in work than when we are unemployed for this to be seen to be true. We enjoy the routine of the working week, weekends and holidays. We enjoy the company of our workmates. We may also enjoy the comfort of pleasant working conditions. All these features, present or lacking, are part of the 'package deal' when taking employment.

Training and promotion

The existence of company-sponsored facilities for training and acquiring new skills, the prospects of regrading (as to both skill and seniority) and the prospects of promotion are all relevant factors in helping us to decide what job to accept.

Holidays

Another part of the package deal will be the entitlement to paid holidays. You may be entitled to three weeks' holiday on full pay at times you can select; or possibly the company may close down for three weeks, in which case you have to take your paid holiday at that particular time. You may be entitled to more than three weeks. If so, is the extra on full pay, or without pay?

Working hours

Working hours might be entirely suitable for you, or you may deem them to be unsocial, especially if shift work involving nights is involved. Do you get a higher rate of pay for night work?

Does 'flexitime' operate at your place of work? This is a comparatively new system of planning working hours, practicable only in certain conditions, under which you yourself may select, within stated limits, the actual hours in each week that you attend for work, provided you put in the required total number of hours. This may or may not be an advantage to you.

Fringe benefits

There are often other and more tangible benefits, too, usually termed fringe benefits or perquisites ('perks'). Some of these can have real monetary value to you and sometimes, especially if their value is not taxable, go a long way in supplementing your cash wage.

Catering

If your employer operates a staff canteen where you can buy meals at prices well below those in outside establishments, this benefit has a very important effect on the total value of your real wage. If there is no canteen but the employer provides luncheon vouchers that can be used in part payment for meals in cafes, this represents an addition to your total remuneration. Luncheon vouchers are free of tax up to 15½p per day.

Social amenities

Facilities for social and sports clubs and for playing fields are increasingly being offered by large employers, and these can be important factors in the total package of benefits.

Pensions

A most important part of your total remuneration is the value to you of membership of any company pension plan. If you qualify to become a member of such a scheme, whether the company pays all or only a part of the regular contribution required, you should look on your eventual entitlement to pension and other benefits as a form of deferred pay. (*See* Chapter 2 for an assessment of pension schemes.)

Benefits in kind

In some industries employees are entitled to be provided with products of the company at a price below cost or even free of charge. Examples are coal for mine workers, air transport for airline employees, rail transport for railwaymen, discounts on new cars for car workers, hairdressing free of charge for department store assistants, subsidised mortgages for the staff of financial institutions, free petrol, loans for paying school fees, and so on.

Your total remuneration may even include the provision of accommodation, either rent-free or at a lower than market rent (*e.g.* nurses in hostels, farm workers), or the use of company-owned holiday accommodation at low rates. Most large companies provide the use of company cars to members of their management teams, and this is possibly the most valuable perk of all. For executives earning more than a stated amount per year the Inland Revenue now assesses the use of a company car to tax, although the net benefit to the employee is still much greater than he would derive from an addition to his salary of the cash equivalent of the use of the car.

Personal income

Another valuable perk offered by some employers is free membership of group schemes for medical or hospital insurance, enabling employees to obtain private treatment in hospital without charge. Others offer free membership of permanent health insurance schemes (*see* Chapter 12).

Getting paid

Employees are generally paid weekly, fortnightly, every four weeks, or once per calendar month. With every payment the employer is legally obliged to supply a pay slip showing in detail how the amount of take-home pay is worked out. In particular it will show basic pay for the period, overtime, bonuses or commission, and will itemise all the deductions.

Certain deductions have to be made from gross pay. Two compulsory deductions are income tax under the Pay-as-you-earn system (PAYE), and your National Insurance contributions. Income tax is explained in Chapter 3. National Insurance contributions, the rates of which are liable to change in the government's annual budgets, are currently (1980) at the rate of 6.75% of pay from the employee, and 10.2% of pay from the employer. The latter amount, of course, does not appear on the pay slip; the employer has to find that amount from his own resources, together with an additional 3.5% wages tax. Deductions for income tax and National Insurance contributions are likely to reduce take-home pay to around four-fifths of total gross pay when you first start working.

Voluntary deductions

By agreement between employer and employee certain other payments that you choose to make on a voluntary basis may be deducted from your pay and the monies paid over by your employer as directed by you. In the pay slip illustrated in Fig. 1.1 the employee, who has joined the company pension scheme voluntarily, is paying £1.75 per week at present, being 4% of his basic pay, into the pension fund which will provide him with a pension on retirement, additional to the state pension. The fact that the employer also pays a sum equivalent to 6% of the employee's pay into the fund, or such other larger amount as may be needed to 'fund' the required benefits (*see* Chapter 2 on pensions), is not, of course, shown on the pay slip. Any contribution by the employer to your pension benefits is virtually an addition to your total remuneration package, namely, deferred pay.

This particular employee also saves £3 a week in a Save-as-you-earn (SAYE) scheme, and puts £2.50 a week into a holiday fund run by the company. He will be able to withdraw a sum equivalent to 52 multiples of £2.50 from the fund to help pay for his holiday, even though he may not have anything like that amount in the fund at the time of his holiday.

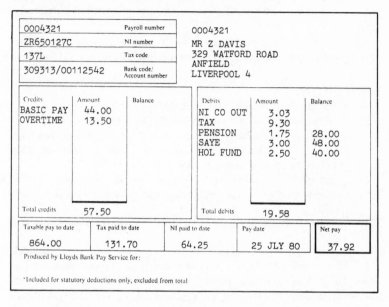

Fig. 1.1

The pay slip in Fig. 1.1, which is reproduced by courtesy of Lloyds Bank Pay Service, is arranged in tabular form – all the amounts due to the employee are on the left, the amounts due from him on the right. Not all slips take this form. Some are printed out by the computer on a long slip, the items being ranged in one or two lines from left to right. But they will still contain the same information, though they may not be so readily comprehensible.

Methods of payment

The traditional method of paying wage earners is for the employees to queue up at a stated time at the pay office and draw their net take-home pay in cash, either loose or, more usually, in a sealed wage packet, accompanied by the pay slip. The law requires that no other method of payment may be used for paying wages to manual workers without the consent of the employees concerned.

Most large employers, and many smaller ones, offer alternative method of paying wages which you are free to accept or decline. These methods avoid the need for handling cash by making payment in one of two ways. Either you may be handed a cheque, which you can pay in to your own personal bank account if you have one, or can cash at your employer's bank; or you can have the net amount of your pay credited direct to your bank account, in which case you may receive your pay slip from your own bank instead of from your employer.

Payment by cheque or direct bank transfer is almost universal for employees engaged on the basis of an annual salary paid monthly.

TEST QUESTIONS

1. What are the two main bases for calculating pay?
2. Briefly explain the difference between a wage and a salary.
3. Explain what is meant by 'time and a half' in describing overtime rates.
4. Name five conditions under which pure time rates are usually the most satisfactory basis for remuneration.
5. What are the main disadvantages of time rates?
6. Suggest ways in which motivation might be introduced for time workers.
7. In what circumstances are pure piece rates to be preferred to time rates?
8. Briefly describe one method of combining piece work with time work.
9. Name some of the advantages of payment based on measured output.
10. Name some disadvantages of piece rates. On what basis would you recommend that the wages of a railway ticket collector be calculated?
11. Name as many examples as you can of fringe benefits.
12. Apart from cash, in what forms might you be asked to accept payment of your net wages?
13. What statutory deductions must be made from your gross pay?

EXERCISES

A John Jones is offered a choice of terms as a salesman for the products of a company. He may be paid a fixed salary of £3,000 plus commission on his total sales at 5%, or a salary of £4,000 plus commission at 7.5% but only on sales exceeding £50,000 in value per year. Assume that total sales for the year will amount to £70,000 in the first year and £85,000 in the second year.

Which formula will give John the higher total remuneration in the first year? And which in the second year?

B Jan Peters, who is very interested in and knowledgeable about electronics, has a choice of two jobs. One is with a branch of a multiple retail chain selling radios, TV sets, music centres, etc. She would receive a weekly wage of £48 for a 40-hour week. No overtime is worked, but once a month the branch staff share, in proportion to their basic pay, a bonus of 3% of total branch sales in the preceding month. Jan's basic wage will be precisely one-tenth of total branch wages.

The branch manager has told her that the value of sales is averaging

£56,000 a month. No specific training is given as the job is largely selling and customer relations. Young assistants qualify by merit, at the manager's discretion, for seniority rises in pay of up to £5 a week each year. Two weeks' paid holiday is allowed, for which the employee would also qualify for his sales commission. Jan would take three weeks' holiday so would forfeit pay and commission for the extra week. Prospects for promotion to branch manager are small.

The other job is that of management trainee with a medium-sized local electronics manufacturing company. Starting salary would be £4,000 per annum. Comprehensive formal training is given during company time and with her ability Jan feels she could expect to be appointed an administrative assistant on the technical development side in a year's time on a salary of £5,500. There is no overtime, bonus or commission, but the company operates a modest pension scheme, supplementary to the state scheme, of which Jan would become a member. The company itself, from its own resources, pays into the fund a sum equivalent to 8% of each employee's salary, the employee contributing nothing. Three weeks' paid holiday is the annual entitlement.

Ignoring the effects of inflation on both pay and prices,

(*a*)   calculate approximate total value of remuneration before tax from each job for the first year of employment;

(*b*)   without detailed calculations, say which job seems likely to pay the higher total remuneration for the second year, briefly stating what factors you take into consideration in making your decision.

2 Pensions

It is hard for a young person just starting work to acquire any sort of enthusiasm for comprehending pension plans. What is going to happen upon his or her retirement 40 or so years later seems too remote a prospect for it to have any relevance in the present.

But such an attitude is unwise, for you will be involved, like it or not, in helping to pay for pensions as soon as you start work. If you become a member of a company pension scheme you will probably be paying towards the cost of your own eventual pension throughout your working life. And, as far as the state pension is concerned, part of your gross wages every week will be deducted from your pay in National Insurance contributions and will go towards the cost of the state pension for today's old-age pensioners.

So you ought to know, as soon as you start full-time employment, roughly what amount of pension you are going to be entitled to and, just as important, who is going to contribute towards its cost and what that cost will be.

Pensions are a complex subject, but taken slowly, step by step, the principles involved are easy to understand. There are two entirely different kinds of pension – the state pension and the so-called occupational pension. Let us deal with these in turn.

The state pension

All persons in paid employment and with a satisfactory record of National Insurance contributions become entitled to the state pension on retirement at age 65 if a man, or 60 if a woman. The state pension consists of two parts – the basic flat-rate pension and the earnings-related additional pension. Both parts are protected against inflation, and the earnings-related part will be based on the pensioner's actual average earnings before retirement.

Basic state pension

For the year November 1980 to November 1981 the flat-rate state pension for a single person is £27.15 per week. For a married couple where the wife's pension is based on her husband's National Insurance contributions the weekly rate is £43.45. Had the wife been in employment and paying full-rate National Insurance contributions in her own right, the joint flat-rate pension would be higher.

The amount of the basic state pension is increased annually at least in line with the general rise in prices. For example, for the year preceding 1980/81 the figures were £23.20 (single person) and £37.30 (married couple).

Earnings-related additional pension

Since the basic state pension is a flat rate, the amount is the same for everybody; it is unrelated to the level of earnings before retirement. But the additional pension introduced in April 1978 *is* related to earnings. This is how it is calculated.

First of all, the government has to set, each year, two levels of weekly earnings as yardsticks against which to assess pension rate. One figure is what is called the 'lower earnings level', and it generally approximates to the rate of the single person's state basic pension. From April 1980 to April 1981 it was set at £23 a week. In April 1981 it will rise to £27 a week to make it approximately the same level as basic state pension.

The other figure, the 'upper earnings level', is set at approximately seven times the lower level. From April 1980 it was £165. These two figures are liable to change each year, as already stated.

Now, for the purpose of calculating the amount of your earnings that is to qualify for state earnings-related pension, all earnings below the lower earnings level are ignored, since the basic state pension will already represent 100% of this amount, at least. And earnings exceeding the upper earnings level are also ignored, since it is considered that anybody with an income of that size ought to look after himself in respect of pension on the excess! That leaves us with the qualifying range of pensionable earnings–in 1981 from £27 to £200 per week.

Your earnings-related pension will be worked out as 1/80th of your weekly pay between £27 and £200 (or such other levels as may be determined each year) for each year of your working life, subject to a maximum earnings-related pension of 20/80ths, or one quarter, of your average qualifying earnings between the two earnings levels.

Of course, you have to contribute towards the cost of your pension in National Insurance contributions, and these are discussed later in this chapter. To qualify for the full 20/80ths of earnings-related pension you will need to have contributed for 20 years from April 1978.

If, by retirement date, you have contributed for *more* than the qualifying 20 years – and most people starting work today will come into this category – you cannot get more than 20/80ths, but the arithmetic will be done on those 20 years which, after each year's pay has been revalued to its equivalent in then current money, will give you the best pension.

Example

A person with a full contribution record, and whose earnings over the best 20 years have been equivalent to an average of £97.50 a week in current terms would, when he retired, get a pension as follows (assuming that the lower and upper earnings levels are unchanged, which is of course unrealistic):

	£
Basic pension	27.15
Additional pension of one quarter of the remainder of weekly pay above the lower earnings level, *i.e.* ¼ × £70.50 (£97.50 – £27)	£17.62
	£44.77

If this person were a married man whose wife relied on his contributions, an additional pension would be payable of £16.30 a week, the difference between single and married rate basic pension.

Self-employed persons qualify for the basic state pension only; they have no entitlement to any earnings-related pension. Their National Insurance contributions, of course, are calculated on a different basis.

Who pays for the state pension?

The state pension, both basic and earnings-related portions, is paid for jointly by all employers in the United Kingdom and by all employees whose earnings are above the lower earnings level, by contributions to the National Insurance Fund, plus a subsidy element from government revenue. The fund is designed to be self-financing in that current payments into it (contributions plus subsidy) are used for making current payments to pensioners, as well as for the other social security cash benefits such as unemployment pay, sickness pay, maternity benefits, and certain others. Amounts of pensions being paid at present (1980) are relatively small when compared with the amounts that will be due for payment after the earnings-related scheme has been in force for a number of years. By 1998 payments will have risen prodigiously since most people then retiring will qualify for the full 20/80ths of average earnings.

National Insurance contributions

Contributions to the National Insurance Fund have to be made in respect of every employed person in the United Kingdom earning not less than the lower earnings level. Both employee and employer have to make contributions. The full rate payable by the employee during the year 1981/82 will be 7.75% of his total earnings up to the upper earnings level (no contributions being payable on the excess), and the full rate payable by the employer will stay at 10.2%.

It appears likely that these rates of contribution may prove to be inadequate in future years, when total pensions payments will have become a much larger proportion of total national income than they are at present. For purposes of tax liability all contributions paid by the employer are, of course, a charge against his profits before tax since they are a business expense (namely part of the cost of labour); but an employee's contributions are not allowable as deduction from an individual's income. He therefore has to pay tax on the amount of his contribution even though he never sees the money.

Occupational pensions

Quite apart from the state pension scheme there are several other ways of providing retirement income by way of pension. They are generally referred to as 'occupational' pension schemes because they are usually connected with or run by the employer.

There are many different types of occupational scheme. One convenient way of categorising them is to differentiate between those which aim to provide benefits of specified or determinable values (these are termed 'benefit-related schemes') and those in which the contributions are predetermined, the members of the scheme having to accept in benefits whatever can be bought in the market with the accumulated contributions (these are termed 'money-purchase schemes').

Benefit-related schemes

More than 11 million people are members of occupational pension schemes of the benefit-related type. These are schemes set up by employers to provide pension and life assurance benefits for their employees in addition to those under the National Insurance scheme.

The most common ways of calculating pensions are either as a percentage of 'final' earnings before retirement or, less commonly, as a percentage of average earnings throughout service.

Average-earnings basis

This basis may be explained by means of a table showing, year by year, the amount of pension that has been earned in that year in accordance with the level of earnings. For the purposes of the example below employees have been placed in 'classes' representing their income range.

Example

Class	Annual earnings	Annual pension for each year	Employee's weekly contribution	Life assurance benefits
	£	£	£	£
A	not over 1,500	30	1.50	3,000
B	1,500 – 1,750	35	1.75	3,500
C	1,750 – 2,000	40	2.00	4,000
D	2,000 – 2,250	45	2.25	4,500
E	2,250 – 2,500	50	2.50	5,000
F	2,500 – 2,750	55	2.75	5,500
G	2,750 – 3,000	60	3.00	6,000
H	3,000 – 3,500	70	3.50	7,000
J	over 3,500	80	4.00	8,000

Note Contributions are not a precise percentage of earnings, but rise in steps. Average percentage in this example is around 5.5%.

If you have been a member of this scheme for 20 years before retiring and your earnings have been as follows, then this is how to calculate your pension:

4 years at £1,600 = 4 × 35 =	£140 p.a. pension
4 years at £1,800 = 4 × 40 =	£160
4 years at £2,300 = 4 × 50 =	£200
4 years at £2,800 = 4 × 60 =	£240
4 years at £3,200 = 4 × 70 =	£280
	———
Total pension earned =	£1,020

This table is only an example; no two schemes are exactly alike. Some schemes, for instance, revalue each year's salary to take account of inflation over the period since it was earned.

Final-earnings basis

A final pay or final salary scheme provides a pension which is a proportion of final pay at or shortly before retirement. The proportion is calculated by allotting a percentage or fraction of final pay for each year of service, so that the pension will usually be larger than with an unrevalued average earnings scheme. Moreover, since most people's real salary rises with age, a final salary is usually a better basis than average salaries revalued.

Example

You are entitled to a pension of 1.25% of final salary for each year of your service up to a maximum of 40 years. You retire after 20 years' service. Your pension will be:

  20 × 1.25% (a total of 25%) of final pay.

Had the fraction been 1/60th, and if you had completed 30 years' service, your pension would be 30/60ths or half final pay.

It is important to look at how 'final pay' is defined in your company's pension rules. It may be defined in one of many different ways, such as earnings in the last complete year of service, or average over the last three years, or the average of the best three out of the last five years, and so on.

Retirement age

Pension schemes will stipulate a certain age at which you qualify for a pension. The usual ages are 65 or 60 for men and 60 or 55 for women.

Is the pension fixed or escalating after retirement?

If the cost of living keeps on rising after you retire, your pension, if it is a static sum, will become less valuable in terms of spending power each year. Many pension schemes provide that pensions, once in issue, shall rise by a stated percentage (3% or 5% is common). Obviously a pension that is escalating has to start at a much lower level than a static one. Alternatively, or even additionally, the managers of the pension fund might increase pensions beyond these figures providing sufficient money is available in the pension fund. Frequently the employer will plough extra money from current profits into the fund to enable such increases to be made.

What benefits are provided?

A good occupational pension scheme provides benefits additional to a pension for you at retirement. For example, if after your retirement you should predecease your wife, she may be entitled to a pension for her lifetime, commonly at half the rate of your pension. There will probably also be benefits payable should you die before retirement. These may take any or all of the following forms:

(*a*)   a refund of some or all of your own contributions;

(*b*)   a single tax-free lump sum payment of up to four times your annual salary;

(*c*)   a pension for your widow.

The table on page 18 illustrates a lump-sum payment for death in service, but not a life pension, to the widow.

Unfunded schemes

The payment of pensions by a company to its retired employees can clearly be very expensive to the employer. In the old days, before pension funds became an established part of the pattern of employment, it used to be common for small firms or companies to pay modest pensions to their retired staff as an act of grace, not as an obligation, and of course these pensions had to be paid for out of profits earned by the business *after* an employee's retirement.

If the company encountered hard times, became insolvent or went out of business, the pension disappeared. No fund had been set up out of which to pay pensions. Such plans are said to be *unfunded*.

There are, even today, some unfunded schemes, but most of them are in the public sector where the payer of the pensions can fall back on current taxpayers for any money required to pay for the pensions. Thus we have the state pension, which is funded only partly by the pay-as-you-earn National Insurance contributions, for these are sufficient only to pay *present* pensions, not future ones. Pensions in later years will have to be paid for from future NI contributions supplemented in all probability by taxation. There is also the Civil Service pension scheme, under which nobody makes any 'pension contributions', the entire cost of the pensions as they fall due for payment, including the linking of them to the Retail Price Index, having to be a charge against future tax revenue. There is no fund. On the other hand many schemes in the public sector (*e.g.* Post Office Superannuation) are completely funded.

Funded schemes

A funded pension scheme is one in which a capital fund is built up over the years from regular contributions intended to be sufficient, with its income generated, to provide enough money for the pensions as and when they fall due. Projected input to the fund is planned to equal projected outgo. That is the true meaning of funding; but the term, in pensions parlance, usually implies two other features. First, that there is a person or organisation behind the fund (usually the employer) who undertakes to provide, from time to time as recommended by the actuaries to the fund, such further contributions to the fund as will be required to honour pension commitments. Secondly, that the fund itself is outside the disposition of the employer, in other words that the assets of the fund are in the ownership not of the employer but of independent trustees – thus even the bankruptcy of an employer could not cause the fund assets to be diverted to other uses.

Contributions

An occupational pension scheme may be either *contributory* or *non-contributory*. Make no mistake over these technical terms, every funded pension scheme requires contributions. But if all the contributions are made by the employer, nothing being required from employees, it is said to be non-contributory, as indeed it is from the employee's point of view. If the employee also has to pay towards the cost it is said to be a contributory scheme.

The state pension scheme is contributory. The Civil Service scheme is non-contributory. Many large employers in the private sector still have non-contributory schemes – and these of course are a particularly valuable 'perk' for employees – but most are now contributory.

The amount that an employer contributes into a pension fund of which you are a member may notionally be thought of as part of your total package of remuneration, for only you and your family can benefit from it. Cases do arise, therefore, where employment at a marginally lower wage from a company that operates a generous pension plan may be preferred to a higher wage with no company pension.

Contributions from employee. In a contributory, benefit-related, pension scheme it is now usual for contributions to be required from members of the scheme at a stated percentage rate of pay. A common rate might be 4% or 5%. From each payment of your wage or salary, therefore, that percentage of pensionable pay will be

21

deducted as pension contributions. These contributions are allowable for tax relief at the top rate of tax payable by the individual, in contrast with NI contributions, which are not allowable for tax relief. To a basic-rate taxpayer each £100 of contribution to an occupational pension plan costs in real terms, therefore, only £70 if he is liable to a top rate of tax of 30%.

Contributions from employer. Contributions from the employer are generally a great deal higher than those from the employee. An employer's contribution could be from 7% to 10% of wages. In a final-earnings pension scheme the size of the employer's contributions in the future is, in fact, unpredictable. This is because, since the employee's rate of contribution is fixed, the employer himself will have to bear the balance of whatever the cost of the benefits turns out to be. Thus in a final-earnings scheme the employer's liability is open-ended. This is in direct contrast with a 'money-purchase' scheme, where the employer knows precisely what his contributions are going to be, as a proportion of total cost of wages, but where the retiring employee has to accept as benefits whatever the accumulated contributions in his name will buy.

Commutation rights

The rules of most private sector occupational pension plans allow a member on retirement to take a single tax-free capital sum in cash from the fund, forfeiting in exchange a proportion of pension. This operation is termed 'commuting' part of the pension. This option may or may not be to the member's advantage, depending on whether at that time he is able to buy with the capital sum better pension benefits in the life assurance market than he is forfeiting in the company scheme. This will largely depend on the rate of interest and of annuities prevailing at the time. In comparing pension forfeited with pension that can be bought with the commuted capital sum, it must be borne in mind that if it is the practice for the employer to increase pension payments partly or wholly to offset inflation, this might prove to be a very valuable feature in the future, and one which could not possibly be provided by any pension bought in the market.

On leaving the employment

All occupational pension schemes must, by law, provide certain minimum rights on leaving the service of the employer. Discussions are taking place during 1980 with a view to making further improvements to these rights.

It used to be possible for a person leaving the service of an employer to be handed back in cash all the contributions he had made to the pension fund. For people now starting work this option is not always possible. The following are the existing alternative rights.

1. The right to a pension, based either on your own contributions to date, or on both your and your employer's contributions, is preserved for you, frozen ready for payment at retirement age.
2. Should you enter the employment of another company that operates a pension scheme, it may be possible for your pension rights to be transferred to the new employer's fund.

In the case of option 2 it will be necessary for both funds to agree to the transfer and for a single capital sum to be transferred from the old fund to the new one. In practice it is often found that some loss in rights takes place. If you elect for option 1 you will eventually receive *two* occupational pensions, one from each fund, and usually the total of the two pensions will be less than it would have been had you remained with one employer and enjoyed the same career structure (assuming the plans to be identical).

Example
If you serve for 20 years with one employer, leaving while earning £6,000, your preserved pension might be, for example, 20/60ths of £6,000, which is £2,000. If your next 20 years are with another employer operating an exactly similar scheme, and if your final salary at retirement is £18,000, your pension from the second employer's fund will be 20/60ths of £18,000, which is £6,000. Total of both pensions will be £8,000. Had you enjoyed the same career and salary structure with a single employer your pension would have been 40/60ths of £18,000, which is £12,000.

The problems involved in transferability of pension rights are vexed ones and cannot be solved without pensions costing a great deal more than they do at present.

Contracting out
Suppose that you are a member of a contributory funded group pension scheme, and that you are contributing 5% of your pay and the employer 10% – a total of 15%.

Bear in mind that both you and your employer are also making contributions towards benefits under the state pension plan, and that these are, in 1981/82, at a combined rate of 17.95% (7.75% + 10.2%). Now, since the government recognises that many people are already in good occupational pension schemes it may be possible for your company pension scheme to be arranged as an alternative to, instead of as an addition to, the state earnings-related scheme. In such a case your employer may have all the employees in his scheme 'contracted out' of the state scheme. In order to be able to do so he must show that his scheme conforms with very stringent conditions, in particular that it guarantees a minimum pension for you that at least matches what you would have got under the state earnings-related scheme, and also some minimum widow's benefits. Most large company group schemes provide benefits far higher than those from the state scheme, and so employees are contracted out. This means that, whereas they will not qualify for the state earnings-related pension, they will pay National Insurance contributions at a significantly lower rate than those quoted on page 17.

Inflation proofing

Even though your company pension may be planned to increase during payment by a stipulated percentage, say 3% or 5% a year, this sort of increase now seems most unlikely to be sufficient for the pension to maintain its spending power if inflation continues at anything like the rate of recent years. There is just no way in which a pension fund can guarantee an inflation-proofed pension, since it is impossible to predict what will be the future rate of inflation. The only organisation that can offer inflation proofing, or index linking as it is sometimes called, is the government itself, for only the government has the power to call upon future taxpayers to provide the necessary funds.

Accordingly, when an employer has contracted you out of the state scheme the *government itself* will protect against price rises part of your company pension up to the amount of earnings-related state pension you would have received had you not been contracted out.

Money-purchase schemes

A money-purchase pension scheme is a very different animal from a final-earnings scheme. By the money-purchase method a stated percentage of your earnings is paid into a pension fund each year, which builds up through reinvested interest and capital appreciation. On your retirement the share of the fund represented by contributions in your name is used to buy an annuity or pension for you.

In some cases these pension schemes are non-contributory (*i.e.*

the cost is all borne by the employer), but in most cases contributions are made by both employee and employer. Such schemes are usually managed either by a life assurance company or by a firm of professional pension managers. If the pension benefits are insured the contributions are used for paying premiums on a group pension policy, the policy being issued to the trustees of the scheme.

A money-purchase pension scheme is often set up for single individuals, and this method is very common in small firms or companies with only five or six employees. In such cases the contributions might be expressed not as a percentage of salary but as a fixed level amount. If a contribution is a fixed amount it will be necessary for an additional policy to be written every few years in order to keep your contributions and pension rights more or less in line with your higher salary.

Pension schemes under the money-purchase method cannot qualify for contracting members out of the state scheme.

The essential difference between the final-earnings method and the money-purchase method is that with the latter the *cost* is fixed, the extent of the benefits being determined by whatever can be bought in the market with the available money at the relevant time; whereas with the former the extent of the *benefits* is fixed (or if not fixed is determinable), the cost to the employer being whatever is needed to attain the required result in benefits. It is impossible for a money-purchase pension to be related to earnings.

Contributions to a money-purchase scheme are allowable for tax relief, as with a final-earnings scheme.

Other benefits

Widow's pension and death-in-service benefits can be included in money-purchase schemes exactly as with final-earnings schemes.

On leaving the employment

Changing employers does not present quite such a problem over pension rights under a money-purchase scheme as with a final-earnings scheme. The following options are usually available.

1. Your rights under the scheme to date may be preserved for payment on retirement, the pensions policy (if one has been issued) being made paid-up.

2. If a pension policy has been issued it may be transferred from the old employer to the new, providing he is willing to continue it in its present form or in some modified form.

3. Should you join an employer who offers no pension plan at all, you may continue the pension policy in your own right, paying all the premiums yourself. But the Inland Revenue rules require that the premiums be actually paid in the first instance by the employer, who can recover the cost from you by deduction from salary.

Pertinent points of a pension plan

Here is a list of some of the questions you will need to ask about any pension plan that may be offered to you as a part of your terms of employment.

1. Who is qualified to join, and at what age?
2. Is it a benefit-related or a money-purchase plan?
3. From what age is the pension payable?
4. Is the plan funded in the sense that pensions are paid out of a fund that is outside the control of the employer?
5. If it is a benefit-related scheme, has the employer undertaken to finance the fund so that it shall always be sufficient to pay all projected benefits as they fall due for payment?
6. If benefit-related, what is the formula for determining the amount of your pension?
7. If the basis is final-earnings, how is this term defined?
8. Is there a pension for the widow of a member who dies after his retirement but before his wife? How is it calculated?
9. What life assurance benefits are payable should a member die before retirement?
10. What provision is there for any increase in pension when once in issue?
11. Is membership compulsory or optional?
12. Is it contributory or non-contributory?
13. Are there any commutation rights?
14. What options are available when members leave the service of the employer?
15. Will members be contracted out of the state earnings-related pension scheme, or will the company pension be in addition to the earnings-related state pension?

TEST QUESTIONS
1. Discover to what figure the basic state pension has been raised.
2. What is excluded from a person's average earnings in assessing the state earnings-related pension?

3. Who pays for the state pension?
4. Discover the present percentage figure of current earnings required to be paid in National Insurance contributions by employees and by employers.
5. If inflation continues after your retirement will the real value of your state pension fall?
6. What is meant by an occupational pension scheme?
7. Distinguish between a benefit-related and a money-purchase scheme.
8. In a benefit-related scheme, describe two bases on which the pension benefit may be calculated.
9. What benefits may be included in any occupational pension scheme other than a pension for your own lifetime?
10. Explain why an employer's liability for contributions to a final-earnings group pension scheme is open-ended.
11. Mention the three main features of a fully funded pension scheme.
12. Why is a money-purchase scheme likely to be less costly to an employer than a benefit-related scheme?
13. Explain the options available to you regarding your company pension rights on changing jobs (*a*) in a group benefit-related scheme, and (*b*) in a money-purchase scheme.
14. Explain the significance of being contracted out of the earnings-related state pension.

EXERCISES

A You earn £3,000 a year and pay income tax at basic rate. You contribute 4% of your gross pay to a company pension plan. You will not be contracted out of the state scheme so will pay full NI contributions. By how much will your net after-tax monthly take-home pay be lower than it would have been had you *not* been a member of the company pension scheme?

B What are the main questions you will need to ask about the company pension scheme of which you would become a member on first taking up employment with a company?

C A member of a fully-funded occupational pension plan, you have been contracted out of the state earnings-related scheme. You have heard it said that you might be at a disadvantage on retirement should inflation continue at a high level, since you will have forfeited part of your state pension which was inflation-proofed by the state. Is this true?

D Jill Mortimer continues working full-time until her retirement at age 60. She is unmarried. During 40 years she has paid the full rate of National Insurance contributions. How will her state retirement pension be calculated?

E Jack Martindale is earning £6,500 a year with a company that operates no occupational pension plan. How much does he pay in a year in National

Personal income

Insurance contributions? What do the company's contributions come to in a year?

F   After having been a member of your company pension scheme for six years you decide to change jobs and elect to have your present pension rights preserved. The pension fund rules provide that you earn pension rights each year of 1/60th of final salary, this term being defined as the average salary over the last three years of service with the company. Maximum pension is 40/60ths of this. Assuming you earned £4,500, £6,000 and £7,980 respectively in your last three years, what will be the value in today's terms of your preserved pension?

3 Direct taxation

The government is obliged to raise a very considerable revenue each year to meet the enormous costs of providing the services that the public has come to expect. The main source of government revenue is, of course, taxation. It also needs to raise money for capital expenditure, and the proper way of doing this is to borrow the required sums, repaying the borrowed money gradually over the years, and paying interest meanwhile. Nevertheless the government does not necessarily behave in this way – some current expenditure is financed out of money borrowed by the issue of government securities to investors, which would be considered unsound practice in a commercial organisation. Indulged in by a government this action has the consequence of continually increasing the National Debt, which in turn means an ever rising liability of the government to pay interest to the lenders, which can only come from the pockets of the taxpayers of future generations.

Taxation takes two general forms. It is said to be *direct* when it is paid to the Inland Revenue directly by the person who bears the cost of it; and it is said to be *indirect* when the person originally paying the tax to the authorities recovers the cost by passing it on to somebody else. One example of direct tax is income tax: nobody can pass on the cost of his tax deductions to anybody else! An example of indirect tax is the duty payable on hydro-carbon oils: this is paid in the first instance to the authorities by the oil companies, but the cost of it is passed on to the consumers of the petrol and oil by adding it to the retail price.

In this chapter we shall discuss direct tax only, since in its commonest form of income tax the impact is felt by earners of incomes at the time of earning the income. Indirect tax, which we pay only when we spend money, not when we earn it, is dealt with in Part Four of this book.

The budget

Tax rates of all kinds can be changed by the government whenever it likes, provided the necessary legislation is passed by Parliament. In practice the rates of most taxes are set in the government's annual budget which is announced in the spring. The budget is, of course, only a set of proposals by the Chancellor of the Exchequer. They are usually incorporated in the subsequent Finance Bill, but sometimes are subject to amendment before they receive the approval of Parliament and become the Finance Act.

Taxes determined by the Finance Act apply only to a single year, called the 'tax year'. The tax year does not coincide with the calendar year but runs from 6 April to 5 April the following year. So the 1981 budget announces the taxes for the 12 months from 6 April 1981 to 5 April 1982.

Income tax

Everybody who receives an income from whatever source is liable to pay income tax on it unless the income is so very small that it falls below the tax threshold. In practice almost everybody in full-time employment pays tax. The rate is expressed as a percentage of taxable income.

Allowable deductions

From total income certain forms of expenditure may be deducted. The two commonest allowable deductions are as follows.

1. Interest paid in any tax year on amounts borrowed for the purchase or improvement of one's main residence (mortgage interest), up to a maximum of the interest on £25,000 (in the year 1980/81).
2. Employee's contributions to an occupational pension plan that has been approved by the Inland Revenue.

There are other allowable deductions, such as payments made under a deed of covenant, which are of significance only to a small minority of people.

Having subtracted the allowable deductions from gross income, you are left with what may be called *taxable income*. But you still don't pay tax on all of it!

Personal allowances

Everybody is entitled to what are called *personal allowances*, on which tax is not payable. The amounts of these allowances are set in each annual budget. For the tax year 1980/81 they were set as follows.

Single person	£1,375
Married couple	£2,145
Married woman's earnings allowance	£1,375

So the allowance for a married couple, when the wife does not work, is £2,145. If the wife is also in paid employment a further allowance against her income of up to £1,375 is made, but limited to the actual amount she earns. Normally, of course, both incomes of a married couple are assessed to tax jointly.

The above levels of personal allowances are intended only for purposes of illustration. They are likely to be increased each year to keep pace with inflation.

Other allowances

As well as personal allowances certain other reliefs may be claimed in relevant circumstances. These rates, too, are liable to change, but in 1980/81 they included the following.

For single-handed responsibility for children	£770
For sole responsibility for dependent relative	
if claimant a man	£100
if claimant a woman	£145
For a housekeeper	£100
For reliance on daughter or son's services	£55
Blind person	£180
Age allowance (over 65)	
single person	£1,820 maximum
married couple	£2,895 maximum
(in lieu of personal allowances above)	

The age allowance is abated by £2 for every £3 of taxable income exceeding £5,900. Thus if taxable income exceeds £6,567.50 (for a single person) or £7,025 (for a married couple) there is no benefit from claiming this allowance.

Your allowances are deductible from taxable income to arrive at a figure for *net taxable income*. The actual tax due is then calculated as a percentage of this.

Rates of tax

Taxable income was charged to tax in the year 1980/81 at the following rates:

> first £11,250 at 30%
> next £2,000 at 40%
> next £3,000 at 45%
> next £5,000 at 50%
> next £5,000 at 55%
> Total £27,500

Net taxable income exceeding £27,500 was charged at 60%.

You will see that income tax rates are arranged so that the tax is *progressive*; that is to say, the proportion of income taken in tax rises as the income rises – in other words, the rich not only pay more but pay *proportionately* more. The purpose of this feature is twofold: it seeks to equalise the burden of tax between rich and poor, the rich being better able to spare a greater proportion of their income in tax; and it seeks to achieve a certain amount of redistribution of income between rich and poor.

There is, however, an obverse to this view. The higher the marginal tax rate the higher the pay rise needed to induce a high-ranking executive to accept more responsibility. Some people argue that very high tax rates may in the past have been responsible for the remarkably high salaries being paid to leaders of industry. It is, after all, the net take-home pay after tax that will induce a person to accept promotion. If the major part of any pay rise is to disappear in tax he may seek a £10,000 rise to persuade him to take a better job instead of, say, a £4,000 rise.

It will be readily apparent that the vast majority of people pay income tax at 30% (this is called the 'basic rate'). Higher rates of tax apply only to the very high earners.

Example A

		£
Pay received in tax year		
39 weeks at £52	£2,028	
13 weeks at £60	780	2,808
Less allowance for single person	1,375	
Net taxable income		1,433

Tax payable: £1,433 at 30% = £429.00 due for the tax year 1980/81.
Weekly PAYE deductions should be about £8.26.

Example B

	£	£
Pay received in tax year		
12 monthly amounts of £1,400 gross		16,800
Wife's part-time earnings		900
Interest on bank deposit account		1,212
Total income		18,912
less Allowable deductions:		
Interest paid on building society mortage of £20,000	3,300	
Employee's contributions to company pension plan	840	4,140
Taxable income		14,772
less Personal allowances:		
married rate	2,145	
wife's earned income allowance	900	3,045
Net taxable income		11,727

	£
Tax payable: £11,250 at 30%	3,375
£ 477 at 40%	190.80
Total tax	3,565.80 for the tax year 1980/81

Investment income surcharge

All forms of income are liable to tax unless they have been specifically exempted (for example, unemployment benefit, and the growth yield on National Savings Certificates – *see* Chapter 4). Thus income from most forms of investment is taxable along with earned income.

Where the income from investment exceeds £5,500 in the tax year the excess investment income is chargeable to an additional 15% tax on top of the ordinary income tax. This is the investment income surcharge. The £5,500 threshold could well change in the future.

Example

James Howard is a widower living alone but employing a housekeeper. His income consists of the state basic pension (no earnings-related pension), an occupational pension of £2,000 a year, and gross income from UK investments, none of which is tax exempt, of £7,200. He pays £730 a year in mortgage interest.

Personal income

In the summer of 1980 he estimates his tax liability for the current year as follows, ignoring the fact that the rate of basic state pension will rise in November and using the existing figure of £23.20 per week. Check his calculations.

	£
State pension	1,206
Company pension	2,000
Investments	7,200
Total income	10,406
less Mortgage interest	730
Taxable income	9,676

less Allowances:		
Single person's	£1,375	
Housekeeper	£100	1,475
Net taxable income		8,201

Tax payable £8,201 at 30%

	2,460.30
plus Surcharge at 15% on £1,700 of investment income	255
	2,715.30

(No purpose is served in claiming age allowance.)

Pay-as-you-earn

An amount in respect of each employee's tax liability has to be deducted by the employer from each payment of wages or salary. This is called the pay-as-you-earn system (PAYE).

In order to ensure that the PAYE deductions are correct it is up to each employee to inform the Inspector of Taxes for the district in which the employer's business is situated what allowances and reliefs he or she is entitled to. The proper way of doing this is to fill in a return of income form and send it to the Inspector. At the end of each tax year the employer himself has to inform the Inspector of the amounts he has paid to each employee and so, if you have no other income and the only allowance you are entitled to is the allowance for a single person, the correct deductions will continue to be made from your pay anyway, so you may not need to do anything. But if the Inspector should send you an income tax return form you must fill it in, sign it and send it back.

The Inspector of Taxes works out, from the information he has been supplied with, a 'tax code'. He sends to you a Notice of Coding, showing how the code has been calculated and this gives you an opportunity for checking that the coding is correct. The code consists of a number and a letter. The number is the total of all your allowances with the last digit omitted. The Inspector also informs your employer of your code number, but *not* how it has been arrived at, since that is confidential. From the code your employer knows precisely how much he must deduct from each payment of your wages to ensure that, by the end of the tax year, you will have paid in tax just about as much as you ought to have done. The employer, of course, hands over to the Inland Revenue all the money he collects under PAYE.

Corporation tax

Limited companies and certain other corporate persons that receive an income have to pay a direct tax called corporation tax on the profits they earn. The rate of this tax in the tax year 1980/81 was 52% of taxable profits, with special provisions for lower rates on profits below a certain figure, whether the profits are made by a small or a large business.

Company profits that are distributed in dividends to shareholders are specially treated. The company must deduct from such dividends an amount equivalent to the basic rate of *income tax,* so that in the hands of the shareholder, where it becomes part of his total income, the dividend is deemed to have been received 'net of basic-rate income tax'. The tax deducted is paid over by the company to the Inland Revenue which treats it, as far as the company is concerned, as an advance payment of corporation tax. In due course the company will have to make further payments of corporation tax, *i.e.* 52% minus 30% of gross profits distributed, and 52% of retained profits, assuming the full rate of corporation tax is payable. There are many allowances that can be made out of profits before tax is chargeable, but these need not concern private individuals. (*See* page 64 for how the dividends are treated for tax in the hand of the shareholders.)

Household rates

A further direct tax, additional to income tax, is payable by all registered occupiers of land and buildings. This takes the form of payment to the local authority in whose area the property is situated. The payments are called 'rates', and this money is required by the local authorities to finance public services and amenities provided locally. These include education, road maintenance, sewers, fire and police services and many others.

The method of assessing rates is quite different from that used in assessing income tax. The amount due is in proportion not to a person's income but to the value of his house. As a wealthy person is likely to occupy a more valuable property, there is thus a link between rates payable and income, but it is a tenuous one. Rates payable are calculated on what is termed 'rateable value' of the house or land occupied by an owner-occupier or a tenant.

Rateable value

The rateable value of a property is intended to represent the amount of annual rent that could be obtained for it in the market if it were let to a tenant, less the estimated cost of maintenance and repairs per year. The actual assessments of properties – the establishing of their rateable values – is normally made at intervals of five years by valuers employed by the Inland Revenue. Since the rateable value is intended to reflect the annual rent, it is meant to bear some relationship to the market value of the property, that is, the sale value of the house. Since properties in different towns, and indeed in different areas of the same town, command different prices on sale because of their location, identical houses may be assessed at different levels.

A rateable value, of course, quickly becomes out of line with real conditions in times of inflation, so that it is almost always lower than the actual rent being paid by the occupier of rented property. Most properties in the United Kingdom were due for revaluation in 1975 but the exercise was not carried out on that occasion. As a consequence most residential assessments are now ten years out of date.

When all the properties in an area have been assessed, the local authority can add together all the rateable values to find the total rateable value of the area. Each year the authority has to budget what it needs to spend on the various services for which it is responsible and determine what income it must acquire to finance this spending. By dividing the amount of the total rateable value of the area by the total income it requires, it determines the level of the current rate demand. For example, with a total rateable value of £5,000,000, and an estimated expenditure in the year of £2,500,000, it will demand rates at 50p in the £.

In addition to the general rate payable to the local authority, a so-called 'water rate' is payable to the authority responsible for the water supply to each property. In some areas the responsibility for sewage disposal has been transferred from the local council to the local water authority, resulting in the 'water rate' being considerably increased. One would expect the general rate to be accordingly lowered, but this in fact seldom takes place, although it may not be raised by as much as it would otherwise have been.

It is quite fallacious to suppose that the keeping of rateable values in a district at a low level can in any way benefit the ratepayers. If rateable values are low then the rate in the £ has to be high. If assessments were to be doubled, the rate in the £ could be halved. In practice, of course, local authorities often find they have to demand higher and higher rates from residents anyway, and the real burden of rates does seem to have been increasing in recent years.

Capital v. revenue expenditure

Local authorities, like the central government, have to spend money on capital projects as well as for current needs such as salaries of the people who provide the local services. Capital expenditure ought, from a strictly accounting point of view, to be financed from capital, since to raise sufficient cash from a rise in the rates to pay for the building of a new school, say, would oblige local householders to bear the entire cost of construction out of their current incomes – whereas the benefits from the expenditure will be enjoyed both by present and by future generations.

It is, therefore, normal for local authorities to borrow money for capital investment either on the money market or by issuing their own bonds or debentures, which members of the public subscribe for in order to get a good yield on their investment. The payments of interest, of course, are a charge against current revenue (income from rates), as also are the repayments of the amount borrowed which may be spread over a long or short period of years as the authority decides.

In contrast to the behaviour of the central government, local authorities seldom finance their current expenditure (sometimes called 'revenue expenditure') from borrowing.

Taxes on capital

For the sake of completeness we must briefly mention two direct taxes on capital, as distinguished from taxes on income, although private individuals are not likely to be burdened with these in the earlier years of their lives.

Capital gains tax

The first is a direct tax that has to be paid on any capital gain made in a tax year on the sale or realisation of an asset. The usual assets involved are investments – both portfolio investments such as stocks and shares and real investments such as investment properties or valuable paintings. Profits realised on the sale of the following are specifically exempt:

(*a*)   your own main residence;

(*b*)   your private car;

(*c*)   British government securities that have been held for over one year (*see* Chapter 5)

(*d*)   most personal chattels.

For the most part only fairly wealthy investors will find themselves having to pay capital gains tax, because the first £3,000 of realised profit in any tax year on the sale of chargeable assets is exempt from the tax anyway.

The rate of capital gains tax in the tax year 1980/81 was 30%. The purpose in introducing this tax was to close a loophole in the income tax laws which had enabled shrewd investors to invest their capital in a form in which they obtained little or no income, which would be subject to tax, but which appreciated in capital value. From time to time they could sell off part of their investment at a profit, which they could then spend as though it were income, yet they paid no tax on it.

In inflationary times the impact of CGT has an unfortunate effect. An investment may grow in value in money terms merely by reason of the fact that the measuring rod, the £, is shrinking, yet the real value of the asset may be unchanged. Thus a share purchased for £100 may be sold after a year for £120, but if inflation has taken place at 20% during that time the holder has made no gain at all. But should he sell the share he will be liable to CGT on the 'profit'.

The provision for exempting the first £3,000 of gain in any year on the sale of chargeable assets is intended to ameliorate the unfairness of this for the small investor.

Capital transfer tax

The old death duties (estate duty) were abolished in 1974/75 and were replaced by capital transfer tax. CTT is designed not only to tax large estates of deceased persons but also to prevent avoidance of such tax by a person's giving away his estate before he dies. CTT is payable both on transfer of assets at death *and* on transfers during life, albeit at a lower rate. It is payable by the recipient unless the transfer is made 'free of CTT'.

Capital transfer tax is a complex subject and here we shall do little more than outline the principles in order to give the reader a complete bird's-eye-view of the entire direct tax structure of the United Kingdom.

The general rule is that transfers of assets by way of lifetime gift or legacy are taxable. The rates of tax are progressive, as are the rates of income tax – higher rates being payable on successive slices of capital – and the progressive rate applies to all transfers commencing from the birth of a person right through to, and including, his death. To determine the tax rate payable one has thus to add together all previous transfers of chargeable assets throughout life.

Exemptions and reliefs. These include the following, although there are others.

1. Transfers of assets between spouses, both during life and at death, are exempt.
2. The first £25,000 of cumulative *chargeable* transfers, year by year during life and at death, is chargeable at a nil rate.
3. Even before (2) above is calculated, the first £2,000 of lifetime gifts *during any tax year* is exempt. One year's allowance, if not used, can be carried forward to the next year, but not to subsequent years.
4. Additionally, the first £100 of gifts *to any one person* in a tax year is exempt.
5. All gifts made out of taxed income and forming part of the normal expenditure pattern such as birthday presents, are exempt.
6. Certain gifts to charities, and in consideration of marriage, are also exempt.

Rates of CTT. On transfers other than those that are exempt, the rate of CTT payable at death starts at 10% and rises to 75% for transfers exceeding £2 million. The rates for lifetime chargeable gifts are half of these rates up to around the £100,000 level, but the abatement in the rate falls thereafter until at £500,000 the rates for lifetime gifts become the same as for gifts at death.

TEST QUESTIONS
1. What is meant by direct, and what is indirect, taxation?
2. What is a tax year?
3. What, in brief, is meant by 'the budget'?
4. What are the two most common deductions that may be made from gross income to arrive at a figure for income that is assessable to income tax?
5. Discover the current rates of personal allowances.
6. Apart from personal allowances, what other allowances may be claimed in appropriate circumstances, and what is the term used to describe the residue of income after deduction of allowances?
7. What is the present basic rate of income tax? Beyond what level of *net taxable income* is tax at higher rates payable?

8. Give examples of income that is exempt for purposes of income tax.
9. What is meant by a 'progressive' tax?
10. What is the investment income surcharge, and in what circumstances is it payable?
11. How is a 'tax code' determined for purposes of PAYE?
12. What is corporation tax?
13. What is meant by the term 'rateable value'?
14. Explain why identical houses and gardens may be allocated different rateable values.
15. Reassessments of properties are made at infrequent intervals. In periods when house prices and market rents are rising rapidly, what effect does this have on the amount of rates actually paid by the householders?
16. To whom are household rates payable?
17. For what purpose are they needed?
18. What is meant by the 'revenue expenditure' of a local authority? How would the construction of a new town hall normally be financed?
19. What are the two direct taxes on capital that mainly apply to private individuals?
20. What capital profits may one make in a tax year without attracting capital gains tax?
21. Give examples of assets on the sale of which a private person will incur no liability for CGT.

EXERCISES

A Harry Pinkerton, a married man, earns £12,700 a year, and his wife earns £4,000, in the tax year 1980/81. There is a mortgage of £15,000 on their home on which they pay interest at 14.5% for the whole of the tax year.

(*a*) What is the net taxable joint income of this couple for the year 1980/81?

(*b*) What is the total tax liability for that year?

B

(*a*) Sarah Jones leaves school and starts work on 6 October 1980. During the tax year to 5 April 1981 she earns a weekly wage of £50.50. Using the rates quoted in this book calculate her taxable income for the tax year and the amount of her tax liability.

(*b*) If she receives a rise in pay of £15 a week after a year's service, and assuming no change in income tax rates but assuming an increase of all personal allowances of 20%, calculate taxable income and tax liability for the year 1981/82.

C John Fraser rents an unfurnished house from the owner on a long lease, paying a rent of £300 a month; tenant is responsible for rates. The rateable value of the property is £462 per annum, the last assessment having been made ten years ago.

(*a*)   Explain the discrepancy between rent payable and rateable value.

(*b*)   If rates are levied at 88p in the £, what will be the amount of rates per year that Mr Fraser will have to pay?

(*c*)   If the 88p rate demand raises a revenue for the local authority of £4,500,000 a year, what increase in rates would be required to raise the total revenue by £1,125,000?

(*d*)   Mr Fraser complains that his friend's house, larger than his and set in a larger garden two miles out of town, has a lower rateable value. Suggest possible explanations for this if (i) the house is in the same local government area; and (ii) the house is in a different area.

PART TWO
Personal investment

4   Money-deposit investments

Apart from the income earned from employment most people receive some modest additional income from money that they have invested. A regular saver builds up quite a useful little nest-egg over the years and the income earned on it can be a welcome addition to his wage. And, of course, the fortunate among us sometimes receive legacies. In this chapter we shall review the various alternatives that exist for depositing our money in such a way that it gives an income yield until we decide where to invest it over the longer term.

When we come to take decisions on where to invest over the longer term, we have to clarify in our minds what we are investing for – what degree of *security* of both income and capital we expect, whether we want to receive the maximum *income flow* from the investment or prefer a smaller income with a *growth in capital value*, and for *how long* we are willing to leave our money tied up. Where we eventually place our money will mostly be determined by the answers to those questions.

For instance, a wealthy man with an already adequate income may invest, not for the purpose of acquiring additional income, but for a growth in the value of his investment; on the other hand a young woman with no capital other than a £1,000 legacy she has received will not want to buy company shares with it, which would be an insecure investment since the value of the shares could go down as well as up; and anybody needing to get his cash back intact in a year's time for the deposit on a house, say, will not place it on a five-year fixed deposit.

Investments that can quickly be converted back to cash with very little or with no cost are said to be 'liquid' investments. The main forms of liquid investment suitable for the private investor are described below.

Banks

Money deposits

Money can be 'lent' or deposited in a variety of ways. The essence of this kind of investment is that you get back in cash your original investment intact – on demand, or after giving the required notice, or at the end of an agreed period. Unlike other forms of investment you cannot transfer or sell your holding to somebody else. Thus these investments are sometimes referred to as 'non-marketable', to distinguish them from those dealt with in Chapters 5 and 6, which can be sold on the market.

Straightforward money deposits, repayable on demand, comprise the most liquid assets of all, other than cash itself. Thus a current bank account on which you can draw cheques is so very liquid that the balance earns no interest at all. But an ordinary account at the National Savings Bank is just as liquid for withdrawals up to £50 a time (of course you cannot draw cheques), and you do earn a modest rate of interest on the balance – 5% in 1980. And as the first £70 of interest a year earned on such an account is entirely tax free, this rate is the equivalent of a 7.1% gross rate where tax has to be paid at basic rate. A warning: interest does not start to be earned until the 1st of the month following the date of deposit and any amounts withdrawn do not earn any interest in the month of withdrawal.

Bank deposit account

Money placed on a seven-day deposit account at any of the commercial banks earns interest at a variable rate, generally 2% below what the banks call their 'base rate'. In July 1980 base rate was 16% so bank deposit rate was 14%. This is gross, and you will have to include the amount of interest earned in your return of income for tax purposes. If you are a basic-rate taxpayer, therefore, the tax-paid yield on a bank deposit account was 9.8% in the summer of 1980.

In theory you are supposed to give seven days' notice for withdrawals, but in practice you can draw out any amount on demand, forfeiting seven days' interest on the amount withdrawn.

Interest is calculated on the daily balance from the day you put your money in.

Fixed-term deposits

Fixed deposits of sums exceeding £10,000 are accepted by the clearing banks for periods ranging from one month to a year at rates ranging from just below to well above bank deposit rate. The reason for the variation in rates is interesting. Remember, the rate is fixed for the whole of the agreed term. If the general level of interest rates in the market were to fall, you are more fortunate in having your money on a long-term deposit than on a short-term one. If the general level of rates were to rise, the reverse would apply. Therefore it follows that in times of high interest levels, when the next change in rates is likely to be downwards, you can expect to be quoted a rather lower fixed rate for a long term than for a short, and vice versa.

Bear in mind that seven-day bank deposits earn a *variable* rate of interest while fixed-term deposits earn a *fixed* rate of interest.

National Savings Bank

As already mentioned, an ordinary account at the National Savings Bank (operated through the post offices) pays only 5% interest. But on an *investment account* at the NSB interest is paid at a higher rate (in 1980 it was 15%). As with the banks, interest is paid gross but is taxable. Again, it is a a variable rate, but the NSB gives one month's notice of any change it is going to make in the rate, whereas banks give no notice. As with all deposits in the NSB, no interest is earned on money in the month in which it is deposited. You have to give one month's notice to withdraw from an investment account so this is not as liquid an investment as some others.

Trustee Savings Banks

A savings account at a TSB earns only 4% gross and there is now no tax relief on the interest. Investment accounts earn more, but the rates vary from region to region throughout the country, the range being from 7% to 14% gross. TSBs also accept money on fixed term at rates between 8% and 14%.

Building societies

Money placed in a building society takes two main forms: it is said to be invested in 'shares' or in 'deposits'. Most people invest in shares and become members of the society. They don't get a share certificate, just a passbook. If you invest in a 'deposit' account you do not become a member of the society and you earn interest at a rate fractionally below the share rate. However, in the case of a liquidation of the society a depositor gets priority over shareholders both for interest and for repayment of capital: thus he has slightly better security. This is hardly an important point nowadays, since the possibility of any loss at all is extremely remote, but at one time it was very important.

If you contemplate one day buying a house and applying for a building society mortgage, then you should certainly become a regular investor in a building society as soon as possible, whatever other savings plans you may have. This is because societies give priority for mortgages to their existing members, and when mortgage money is in short supply you are unlikely to be able to get a mortgage at all unless you've got a good savings record over a number of years with a society.

Interest rates payable on building society investments fluctuate with the market. In the autumn of 1980 most societies were paying 10.5% after tax on ordinary share accounts. For regular savers the rate is usually above the ordinary share account by about 1%. A tax-paid interest rate of 10.5% is quite attractive, since it represents a gross return to a basic rate taxpayer of 15%. Since interest rates in the latter half of 1980 appear to be on the downward path it seems likely that building society rates will shortly fall slightly.

Higher rates

Building societies are in very active competition with banks for the public's spare cash and now offer a wide range of investment plans going under such titles as Subscription Shares, Build-up Shares, and Open-ended Bonds, as well as the traditional fixed-term shares. You can earn from ½% to 2% net above the recommended share rate according to the period of time you are willing to forgo your right to withdraw the cash.

Bear in mind, when choosing a society, that interest rates, both for investors and for borrowers, are higher in some societies than in others. If you are not at all concerned with qualifying for a mortgage one day, then your choice is easy: go to whichever society, being a member of the Building Societies Association, offers you the best rates. Naturally, if you are dealing with a lesser-known society, first check its standing.

Interest tax-paid

A very important feature to bear in mind with *all* money invested in a building society is that the interest is paid to the investor net of tax. For example, ordinary share rate in 1980 was 10.5% from most societies. That means that if you have £100 invested you earn £10.50 a year on it and, if you are liable only to basic rate income tax, you are liable for no further tax on your £10.50.

It is incorrect to say that building society interest is 'tax free'. It isn't: tax has in fact been paid on the interest to the Inland Revenue direct by the society. Incidentally the rate of tax they pay is at a specially favourable rate called the 'composite rate', pitched at a level intended to represent the average tax rate paid by all building society members collectively, including many, of course, who are not liable to tax at all! But in the hands of the investor the income is treated for tax purposes as having already paid basic rate tax. If you have a very large income and are liable to tax on part of it at the higher rates, say at 40%, then the *net* £10.50 interest received from the society must be 'grossed up' to the amount it represents before tax. Simple arithmetic shows that if £10.50 is 70% of the gross amount, then £15 must be the gross before tax figure. You would have to pay another 10% (40% − 30%) tax on the £15.

Tax not reclaimable

No tax can ever be reclaimed on building society interest in any circumstances. This means that for a person with a very small total income that is not in the taxable range at all, investing in a building society may not be a good idea, for he would be effectively paying more tax than he need. If, for example, he were to put his money in a bank deposit account instead of a building society he would get a net yield of 14%, instead of the net 10.5% from the building society.

No fixed rates

It should be borne in mind that the interest rates from building societies are fluctuating ones. Even with fixed-term regular savings and open-ended bond shares, although the margin above share rate is guaranteed for the contracted period, the ordinary share rate on which it is based is not. It is thus important to distinguish these rates from those payable on other fixed deposits such as with a bank, where the rate of interest is fixed for the whole term. This is significant to an investor, for in times of high interest levels, when the next change is more likely to be down than up, a fixed rate could be an advantage should interest rates fall. The reverse also applies.

National Savings Certificates

National Savings Certificates, which can be bought or repaid over the counter of any bank or post office, are a very different animal from other forms of cash deposit investments, for they do not earn interest at all. Instead, their repayment value increases year by year, at an escalating rate, and (most important) their increase in value is *entirely tax free to everybody*.

Comparing the yield on National Savings Certificates from that on other money deposits is a tricky business, for the rate of growth in value starts quite low and builds up to the maximum in the fifth year. The table below illustrates the growth of the 19th issue which was first issued in February 1980. Purchase price is £10.

	Value at the end of year	Yield	Equivalent yield gross to basic-rate taxpayer
1st year	£10.50	5%	7.14%
2nd year	£11.40	8.57%	12.24%
3rd year	£12.45	9.21%	13.16%
4th year	£14.1	13.25%	18.93%
5th year	£16.30	15.95%	22.79%

It will be seen from this table that for a non-taxpayer it does not pay to buy National Savings Certificates unless they are held for the full five years, since 14% interest can be earned on a bank deposit account For a basic-rate taxpayer, however, it could pay him to invest only for four years. The critical period occurs during the fifth year, at the end of which the year's growth rate is at the dramatic level of 22.79%.

As a general guide, therefore, it does not pay to invest in National Savings Certificates unless there is an intention of holding them for five years. The *average* annual compound growth rate over five years works out to 10.33%; since this is tax-free a basic-rate taxpayer would need to obtain a gross yield of 14.75% to compete with it. So long as the bank deposit rate exceeds this figure, however, this is not difficult. So why buy NSCs at all?

The answer is, of course, the same as before: yield on NSCs is guaranteed and would look very attractive in later years if market rates of interest were to fall. And were you to wait for that fall you might be too late, for this issue of NSCs would probably be taken off the market!

Maximum holding permitted per person is £5,000 of certificates of the 19th issue, in addition to any of earlier issues held.

Save-as-you-earn schemes

The government sponsors two special schemes for regular savers which give a return to an investor which might be higher than a commercial organisation could afford, depending on changes in interest rates in the market over the next five years and the rate of inflation over the same period.

SAYE (2nd issue)

This scheme is operated through building societies and the National Savings Bank. You have to enter into a commitment to save from £1 to £20 (the maximum) a month for five years. You receive no payments of interest, but at the end of five years a bonus is added to your investment free of tax. The bonus is equivalent to an annual compound rate of 11.86% to a basic-rate taxpayer.

Your contributions cease at the end of five years, but if you then leave the investment intact for a further two years a second bonus is added, again free of tax. Over the seven years the bonuses are equivalent to a compound interest rate of 12.31% a year gross to a basic-rate taxpayer. If interest rates in the money market were to fall significantly in the near future this could prove to be a worthwhile investment since the return is guaranteed for the whole period.

If you fail to keep your savings commitment during the first year you get neither bonus nor interest, but you get your contributions back. If you drop out after one year but before five years you get no bonus but are paid interest on your contributions at the rate of 6% tax free.

SAYE (3rd issue – index-linked)

The SAYE 3rd issue is much more interesting. You have to contract to save an amount of from £4 to £20 a month for five years. You get neither interest nor bonuses. But the repayment value is linked to the Retail Price Index, so this is an inflation-proofed investment. So long as inflation proceeds at a rate higher than the going net-of-tax interest rate on deposits, this will be impossible to beat for yield.

Again, there are penalties for not keeping to your contract. You get nothing except your original contributions back if you stop before the end of 12 months; stop after a year but before five years and you get no inflation proofing, but you will be paid 6% tax-free interest.

At the end of five years each of your monthly contributions is up-valued in respect of the fall in the value of money during the interval, and you may draw out the up-valued investment. Alternatively you may leave the investment intact for a further two years, still with RPI adjustment, *plus* a tax-free bonus equal to two months' contributions.

Inflation and interest yield

When assessing the security of capital in any investment, whether money-deposit or any other kind, you should bear in mind the consequences of continuing inflation. For example, if you invest £100 on deposit at 15% gross for a year, and draw out the £100 capital at the end of the year, the money at that time will not buy as much as it would have done at the beginning of the year if inflation has been running at, say, 18% during the year. After a year your £100 will be worth only £82 in current money.

To make an investment really worth while from a yield point of view, the interest rate should be sufficient to give you not only a reasonable tax-paid yield in income, but also compensation for loss in value of your capital. To be compensated for a loss of 18% from inflation, you need a tax-paid interest rate of 18% grossed up for tax. At basic-rate income tax this works out at $(18 \div 70 \times 100)$ 25.7%. You would also need some addition to that rate to provide any real return at all. In short, without a gross interest yield of at least 30% there is no prospect of making a real return on investments in 1980 conditions – the best rates are therefore negative.

TEST QUESTIONS
1. What benefits can be looked for from any investment?
2. What do you understand by the term 'liquidity' as applied to an investment?
3. Define the term 'money deposit'.
4. When choosing a method of depositing money what factors would you take into consideration?
5. If the next change in market levels of interest rates is likely to be up rather than down, would you choose to deposit money at a fluctuating rate of interest or a fixed one, other things being equal?
6. Is the interest earned on a building society investment tax-free?
7. In what circumstances is it inadvisable to invest money in a building society?
8. By what means can one obtain interest rates on a building society investment at levels above ordinary share rate?
9. If you are saving in order to build up a sum of money for a single large expenditure in three years' time, would you select National Savings Certificates? Explain your reasons.
10. Describe one method of regular saving and investment where your capital is index-linked.
11. What is understood by a 'negative yield'?
12. Discover by enquiry the current interest rates available on deposits with the commercial banks, in ordinary building society shares, and on

investment accounts at the National Savings Bank. Say which gives the best yield, and explain what considerations other than interest rate should be allowed for in selecting the most suitable for investment.

EXERCISES

A   Lilian Garside, who is liable to basic-rate tax at 30% on her total income, has £2,400 to invest for a period of two years only. Which of the following will give her a better yield?

(*a*)   Two-year term shares in a building society paying 0.75% over ordinary share rate of 8.75%, tax paid.

(*b*)   Bank deposit account on which the interest rate is 11%.

Would she get an even better yield by placing the £2,400 in an ordinary share account in a building society, and drawing out of it £100 a month which she places in a subscription share account paying 2% above ordinary share rate?

B   Jack Fenton decides to save £20 a month merely to provide a liquid reserve which he might want to spend at any time. Would you advise him to place it in SAYE (index-linked), 3rd issue on the grounds that inflation is likely to continue at over 15% a year for several years, or in some other investment? Mention your reasons.

5   Fixed-interest investments

In Chapter 4 we discussed only deposit investments, namely investments that give complete security of the capital and from which you can 'disinvest' simply by drawing the money out – on demand, or after giving the prescribed notice, or at the expiry of the agreed term. With most such investments you do not have certainty of income, for the interest rate can fluctuate up or down. Exceptions to this are National Savings Certificates and SAYE (2nd issue), where you have security of both capital and income, and SAYE (3rd issue, index-linked) where you have absolute security of capital but no income.

In this chapter we shall contrast those investments with others where income is secure but capital value is variable. These are called 'fixed-interest investments', and most of them are marketable – that is to say, you can sell your holding to somebody else on the market, at whatever price it will fetch at that time. You cannot, of course, sell money-deposit investments, which are therefore called 'non-marketable', or 'non-negotiable'.

Government stocks

The largest collection of marketable fixed-interest investments consists of the so-called 'gilt-edged' stock issued by the government. Part of the government's vast expenditure is financed by raising loans from members of the public and the financial institutions such as banks, insurance companies and pension funds, who subscribe cash on loan to the government and receive in exchange a certificate or bond setting out the terms of the stock.

They are called gilt-edged or simple 'gilts' because the security is undoubted, both income and eventual repayment being guaranteed

53

by the government. But since some stocks are not repayable for very many years (indeed, a few are not repayable at all), there *is* an element of risk in capital value for most holders, who would not be willing to wait that long to get their money back and who will, therefore, have to sell on the market.

The various names attached to the different stocks have no significance at all; the stocks are all government-backed borrowings. There is no essential difference between a stock called 'War Loan' and one called 'Treasury Stock' or 'Exchequer Stock'; the names simply help to identify the particular issue. What does have significance are the terms of the issue, and these vary enormously. Three main terms to look for are:

1. *The interest rate.* Traditionally, gilts carry a fixed rate of interest which cannot be varied throughout the life of the loan. Thus one has '3½% War Stock', for example, or '6½% Treasury Stock'. This guaranteed interest rate is sometimes called the 'coupon' or 'coupon rate', a term derived from the fact that a long time ago stocks were issued in the form of bearer bonds that had coupons attached to them that the holder would detach and present for cash each time an interest payment was due. (During 1980 a government stock carrying a variable rate of interest was issued; this experiment will not be discussed here.)

2. *The repayment date.* Most stocks are redeemable (repayable) on a named date, or during a specified year, or between stated dates. Thus one may have '7¼% Exchequer Stock, 1988–90' which the Treasury is bound to repay to the then holders on a date of its own choosing some time during those two years. A very few issues have no redemption date and are therefore irredeemable or perpetual loans.

3. *The repayment terms.* Stocks are normally repayable at par, *i.e.* a holder will get back in cash £100 for each £100 of nominal stock that he holds.

New issues

Issues are being made of new stock all the time, partly to finance the continually increasing need of the government to borrow to finance its spending, and partly to take the place of stocks maturing and being repaid. A subscriber for a new issue must look at a fourth term – the amount payable on issue. This need not be at par (£100 cash for £100 of stock); it could be 'at a premium' (exceptional) or 'at a discount'. For example, a new issue could be made in 1981 of 12½% Treasury Stock 1996 'at 90'. That means that a subscriber will need to invest only £90 in cash to get £100 nominal of the stock, on which he will be paid interest of £12.50 gross (usually payable in half-yearly instalments, and with basic-rate tax deducted) until, 15 years later, the government pays him out at par.

Yield

Notice two main points. The coupon rate is 12½%, so the subscriber gets £12.50 a year interest on an investment costing £90, which works out at a flat or running yield of 13.88%, since 12.5 is 13.88% of 90. The arithmetical formula is very simple:

$$\frac{\text{par value (100)} \times \text{coupon}}{\text{price}} = \text{running yield } \%.$$

But if the subscriber were to hold on to his investment until maturity in 1996 he will make a capital profit of £10 – roughly 66p a year. So the gross *yield to redemption* is:

$$\frac{100 \times (12.5 + 0.66)}{90} = 14.62\%.$$

These calculations make no allowance, of course, for inflationary loss in the value of the capital.

Yield comparisons

The yield on short-dated stocks – those that are due to mature within five years – does tend to reflect the current levels of interest in the short-term money market (itself partly determined by short-term expectations of inflation rate). But the yield on the longer-dated stocks follows more the anticipated long-term average interest rate and long-term expected inflation rate.

Buying and selling

Unlike money-deposit investments, gilt-edged stocks can be bought and sold on the market, daily prices being quoted on the Stock Exchange. Indeed most personal holders of government stock are not the original subscribers but have bought their holdings on the market.

Price changes

The price of a government stock can rise and fall, reflecting falls and rises respectively in the general level of interest rates. For instance, if a long-dated 15% stock were to be issued at par during a period when 15% is the going rate for bank deposits, the issue would probably be fully subscribed, since most people will reckon that rates will go down rather than up and that over the long term the average market interest rate will be a lot lower than 15%.

Now, when interest rates fall, say to 10%, that particular stock becomes very attractive from an investor's point of view, since it continues to pay a fixed £15 of interest a year per £100 of nominal capital. Demand for the stock on the market will immediately tend to drive up its price to around £150, for at that level a holder will get a gross running yield of:

$$\frac{15 \times 100}{150} = 10\%.$$

In practice the price will not reach 150, for as soon as a stock price exceeds par, the holder at redemption will make a capital loss. This loss will have to be discounted over the years in the price.

Comparative prices

The yields on gilt-edged stocks cannot become much out of line with one another, since the security of income and capital is the same in every case. There are, of course, variations arising from differences in redemption dates, the consequence of which have already been explained (*see* page 57 for a detailed calculation). As a very general rule it is good policy to buy gilts when interest rates are high, and sell them when interest rates are low. In this way you buy at a low price and sell at a high price.

Price and redemption yield

Changes in prices are not strictly in inverse proportion to the changes in market interest rates, and this is because any change in price introduces a change in the potential capital loss or gain that the holder will make on redemption. Suppose that a 12% stock, standing precisely at par in 1981, is due for redemption exactly five years later. Suppose further that the interest rate level for five-year money, hitherto at 12%, drops to 10%.

If the price of this stock were to be pushed up by the market to 120, at which level the flat yield would coincide with the 10% market level, the holders would stand to make a capital loss in five years' time of £20 per £100 nominal held – a redemption loss of £4 a year. In practice, therefore, the price will tend to rise only to that point where the *redemption yield* becomes more or less in line with general interest level expectations – in other words, where the running yield less the annual capital loss comes to about 10%. In this case equilibrium will be reached at a price of about 106.5. At this level the flat yield with a coupon of 12% is 11.27%. Allowing for an annual capital loss to redemption of:

$$\frac{6.5}{5} = £1.30, \text{ a percentage rate of } 1.22\% \text{ of } £106.50.$$

the redemption yield is about 10% (11.27 − 1.22).

It will now be realised that when a dated stock is bought at a premium (price above par) the running yield should be higher than the prevailing level of interest rates in order to compensate a holder for his potential capital loss. Conversely, when a dated stock is bought at a discount (price below par) the running yield should be lower than the prevailing interest rate to allow for the potential capital gain.

Example

A 12½% government stock maturing in three years' time is quoted at 91½. Calculate:

(*a*)   the gross income (or flat, or running) yield, and
(*b*)   the gross redemption yield.

Answer

(*a*) $\dfrac{100 \times 12.5}{91.5}$ = 13.66% income or flat or running yield.

(*b*) $\dfrac{100 \times (12.5 + 2.83)}{91.5}$ = 16.75% redemption yield.

Accrued interest

Another reason for the disparity between the yields on stocks that ought, on the face of things, to be identical, is concerned with the due date of the interest that is paid on the holdings. As interest is paid to stockholders at half-yearly intervals it follows that a holder who purchases just after an interest payment will have a full six months to wait for this first interest payment; whereas one who buys five months later will have only one month to go before receiving a full six months' interest. The first purchaser is buying capital only; the second is buying capital plus accrued interest to date. As a general rule, therefore, a 12% stock priced at par will rise in price £1 a month from the date of one interest payment until the day before the next interest payment. It will then drop by £6 to start rising again.

Government stocks are dealt in on the Stock Exchange 'ex-dividend' (buyer not entitled to the interest payment) for the five weeks before the interest due date, to give the Bank of England a chance to get the interest warrants made out and posted to the then registered stockholders. So anybody who buys 'ex-div' gets the capital only, and the price he pays will be proportionately down. One who buys 'cum-div', being entitled to the interest, will pay a correspondingly higher price.

Tax treatment

The interest earned on gilt-edged stocks is, of course, taxable income in the hands of the stockholder. In practice the interest payments are made by the Bank of England, the registrar for most stocks, net of tax at the basic rate of income tax, so the stockholder, unless he is liable to higher rates of income tax or to the investment income surcharge, is not liable to pay any further tax on it. Thus a holder of £1,500 nominal of 8½% stock will receive each half-year an interest warrant for £44.60 net, representing a gross payment of £63.75 (4.25% of £1,500) less tax at 30%.

A very small number of specified stocks (*e.g.* 3½% War Stock) is paid gross, but in the hand of a UK resident this income is taxable.

National Savings Register

Most popular government stocks can be bought and sold in small quantities on the National Savings Register, which is a subsidiary register to the Bank of England. An attraction is that interest payments are made without deduction of income tax – a useful feature for a person whose income is not taxable. Dealing costs are lower than are those attaching to transactions through a stockbroker where the Bank of England main register is used, but prices are less keen.

Capital gains

Capital gains made on sale or redemption of government stock are not, of course, liable to income tax. As far as capital gains tax is concerned they are given special treatment. If a stock is disposed of at a profit within a year of its acquisition, there is a liability to CGT on the gain. But since the first £3,000 of gain in any tax year is exempt anyway, this will not concern most small investors. Profit made on government stock held for over one year is exempt from any CGT liability.

The impact of income tax and CGT was ignored on page 57 when calculating redemption yields, as only gross yields were being discussed. In calculating net after-tax yields allowance must be made for the distinction made in tax liability between income and profit.

Example

£2,000 of 8% stock is bought at 82 by a person liable to basic-rate income tax but not to investment income surcharge, and is sold nine months later at 84, after receipt of two half-yearly interest payments. Calculate the net total after-tax return on the investment expressed as an annual percentage rate on the outlay, ignoring dealing costs.

Answer

Income received (gross)	£160	
less Tax	48	net £112
Capital gain, 20 × 2 (assume no CGT)		40
Total net		£152

Capital invested was £1,640 for three-quarters of a year.
Therefore net return:

$$\frac{152 \times 4 \times 100}{3 \times 1640} = 12.4\% \text{ net return per annum.}$$

Local authority loans

Many local authorities borrow money both in the money market and by public issues in much the same way as the central government. These loans are secured by a charge on the local rates of the authority, which makes them only slightly less secure than government stock. The yields are therefore marginally higher than government gilts.

Some short-dated non-negotiable local authority mortgages can be bought at par direct from the local authority concerned. Longer-dated negotiable loans can be bought and sold on the Stock Exchange on lines similar to those for government stocks.

Limited companies

Some limited companies in the private sector also raise finance on fixed-interest terms, issuing dated debentures repayable on or before a named date, irredeemable debentures, or preference shares which are usually, though not necessarily, irredeemable. Both kinds of investment carry risks for the investor, though debentures are better secured than preference shares since they represent a loan to the company which takes priority both for income and capital over any claims by shareholders of the company. Preference shares, carrying slightly more risk than debentures, yield a slightly higher rate in terms of income.

Costs of dealing

Unlike money-deposit investments, where there is usually no cost either in depositing or withdrawing, the buying and selling of marketable fixed-interest securities does involve certain costs. For government gilt-edged investments they include the following:

Stamp duty on transfer form	Exempt
Contract stamp	10p to 60p on contracts over £100.
Brokerage (commission charged by stockbroker)	At the rate of 0.625% of the contract with a minimum of £4 per transaction between £200 and £640. VAT is payable on this.

TEST QUESTIONS

1.   What is a gilt-edged stock?
2.   In what two ways could you invest in gilt-edged stocks?
3.   Are you sure of getting your money back when buying gilts?
4.   Why are government stocks of identical maturity dates priced at such different levels on the Stock Exchange?
5.   How is the flat income yield calculated on a fixed-interest stock?
6.   What is meant by 'redemption yield'?
7.   What is the main reason for periodic changes in the general level of prices of gilt-edged stocks?
8.   What does the term 'coupon rate' signify?
9.   What are the main advantages and disadvantages from buying gilts on the National Savings Register as opposed to the normal Bank of England Register?
10. What CGT would be payable on a profit made on the sale of a gilt-edged stock?
11. Why do local authority loans give a better income yield than central government gilts?
12. Can one invest in fixed-interest securities in the company sector?

EXERCISES

A   Jonathan Brown has £2,000 to invest. Ignoring brokerage and other charges, which of the following will give him the best income yield?

(a)   9% Treasury Stock priced at 85.
(b)   6½% Funding Stock priced at 70.
(c)   Bank deposit paying 9%.

B   In 1981 Jill White wishes to select a gilt-edged stock for a four-year period. She has the choice of:

(a)   4% Exchequer redeemable at par in 1985, priced at 75.
(b)   7½% Funding redeemable at par in 1989, priced at 84.

Which of these is likely to give a better redemption yield *over the next four years*, ignoring tax considerations?

6   Long-term investments

For the really long-term investor, one who is prepared if necessary to have his capital tied up over a period of many years, a long-dated fixed-interest stock bought at a time when interest rates are at a high level is perfectly suitable. But for him there are also other possibilities not open to a short-term investor.

Equities

The first possibility is to buy ordinary shares of companies – often referred to as 'equities'. These are literally a share in the ownership of companies in the private sector, and are essentially risk capital. The companies make no guarantee to pay dividends on the shares, and there is no certainty that a shareholder will get his capital back. Were the company to lose all its capital, for example, through trading at a loss, through bad management, or from the uncertainties of a changing market for its product, the shares could become practically worthless, and would certainly pay no dividend.

That said, however, the potential for gain is unlimited. Very successful companies are sometimes able to increase their profits and dividends at such a rate that both dividends and market value of the shares can double in quite a short time. Others make losses. Selecting shares to buy is a tricky business and is really a job for the professional investor.

Nominal value

A share in a company is described as having a certain value, *e.g.* £1 share, 50p share, 25p share. Thus if a company has an issued share capital of £10,000,000 there might be 10 million £1 shares, 20 million

50p shares, or 40 million 25p shares, and so on. Although a £1 share will have been worth just £1 when the money was first subscribed for it, it would be purely coincidental were it still to be valued at that figure at any date thereafter; it might be higher, or it might be lower, depending on how profitably the company has been trading.

A holder of 1,000 £1 shares in a company with an issued share capital of 10,000,000 ordinary shares, is technically the owner of one 10,000th part of the company. He does *not* directly own any of the specific assets of the company, but only his share of what is collectively left over after all prior claims have been met. These claims will include those of any loan stock holders, debenture holders, preference shareholders, bankers and trade creditors. What is left is sometimes called 'ordinary shareholders' funds', or just 'the equity'.

When a company makes a profit it is usual for a large proportion of it to be retained in the business to enable it to expand and, in times of high inflation, to maintain the real value of the company's assets; only some of the profits are distributed in dividends. So a company that has been profitably trading for, say, five years may have ploughed back profits as large as the starting capital, and used some of them for expanding the business and making even bigger profits. Although the net assets of the company – that is, the total of assets less the total of outside liabilities – when it started up five years ago may have been of a value of only £10 million, they might now be worth £20 million in today's money. (It may be remarked that the price of a share would need to double in that time merely to retain its real value.)

Market value and growth

One might think from this that a shareholder could sell a share in a company such as that just mentioned for £2 on the market. Although this could be so it is not necessarily so. The price of any share in the market is determined by the actions of buyers and sellers on the Stock Exchange, and most people buy industrial shares not because of their underlying asset value, but for what the shares represent in terms of a flow of income by way of future dividends, and of capital growth (*i.e.* future rises in market price of the shares).

So the market price of a share reflects many factors:

(*a*)   the rate of current dividend distribution;
(*b*)   the anticipated future distribution;
(*c*)   the anticipated trend in pre-tax profits;

(*d*)   the policy of the company in retaining and distributing profits;

(*e*)   the state of the company's balance sheet.

Factors (c) and (d) determine a sixth factor, the prospect for the future of further growth in the net asset value of the shares; and factors (a), (b) and (c) determine a seventh factor, the anticipated future response in the market to that growth. In other words, a widespread belief that the share price will rise will itself create a rise in price.

In general, therefore, company dividends alone represent a fairly low yield expressed as a percentage of the price of the share, since what the investor hopes to obtain from his holding is not so much current income as growth over the longer term. There was a time when the dividend yield on equities was significantly higher than the running yield on gilts; and this was what was then expected, for the ordinary shareholder was risking his money in a business venture whereas the buyer of gilts was merely lending money to the government. But today (1980), with inflation at around 20% and the world economy in recession, industrial profits are not easily earned and the dividend yield on ordinaries is, on average, well below the yield on gilts.

So why do people buy equities? The main urge to do so comes from the belief – which may by perfectly well founded – that over the very long term industry will again become very profitable. When it does so the value or price of shares might well rise by far more than would be needed merely to compensate the holder for his meagre dividends.

Dividends

The dividend that a company pays to its shareholders is a distribution out of current profits net of tax; that is, after allowing for the corporation tax of up to 52% and any overseas taxes the company will have to pay on its profits. If in a given year it makes no profits it is unlikely to pay more than a token dividend. If profits are high it can pay more; if they are low it may have to pay less.

Example

Assume that a company with a share capital of 2,520,000 ordinary 50p shares earns a gross taxable profit in a given year of £183,750. Assume also that the company will be liable to pay a sum of £95,550 to the Inland Revenue in corporation tax (tax is unlikely to be precisely 52%; the tax provisions are very complicated and will not be gone into here). This leaves

63

Personal investment

only £88,200 after-tax profits available for disposal. If the directors decide
to recommend distributing half of this as dividend and to retain the other
half for expanding the business, total dividend distribution will be £44,100.
Divide this by the number of issued shares and the dividend will amount to
'1,75p net per share', *i.e.* a dividend of 3.5% net of tax on the nominal value
of 50p. A shareholder with 1,000 shares wil receive a dividend of £17.50.

Companies normally pay dividends twice a year – an 'interim'
dividend halfway through their financial year, based on estimates of
what the final profits are likely to be, and a 'final' dividend after the
end of the year. In the above example where the total dividend in
the year was 1.75p per share, an interim payment will probably have
been made of around 0.70p leaving a final amount payable of 1.05p.

Tax on dividends

Dividends received by a shareholder have already borne
corporation tax. To avoid tax being paid twice on the same income,
the dividend is treated by the Inland Revenue as though it has paid
basic-rate income tax in the hands of the shareholder. For most
shareholders, therefore, a dividend is 'tax paid' and no more tax will
be payable on it.

On the advice form or 'tax voucher' that the shareholder receives
with his dividend warrant there will be a note of how much 'tax
credit' is associated with the dividend payment. This tax credit is
normally the amount which must be added to the net dividend to
bring the total to a gross (before tax) figure. It is this grossed up
figure (dividend plus tax credit) which will count as part of an
individual's assessable income for tax purposes.

Example
A dividend of £75 is received, and the tax voucher shows a tax credit of
£32.14. The shareholder's gross income from this holding is therefore
£107.14, on which he is deemed to have already paid £32.14 basic-rate tax,
assuming that basic rate is 30%.

It is therefore very important, when considering dividend rates, to
distinguish between the cash dividend, which is the net amount
received after tax, and the dividend plus tax credit, which is the
gross amount. Dividends and yields quoted in the newspapers are
based on the gross figures. On the other hand the voucher that
accompanies the dividend warrant customarily declares the dividend at the net rate of actual cash paid.

Example

Which of the following investments gives, to a person liable only to 30% basic tax, the better flat yield, ignoring all brokerage and other charges?

(*a*)   5% funding stock at a price of 70;
(*b*)   £1 shares priced at 210 paying a net cash dividend of 13p.

Answer:

(*a*)   £70 invested will yield £5 gross, which works out at 7.143% gross;
(*b*)   £2.10 invested yields 13p net. Thus £210 invested would yield £13 net which works out at 6.19%. Since this is a net after 30% tax figure one must divide by 7 and multiply by 10 to give 8.84% gross.

Therefore (*b*) is better.

Prices and yields

It will now be realised that declared rate of dividend and actual rate of yield on the money invested are very different measurements. A published figure of 4p net per share as dividend on a £1 share (or 4% net on the nominal stock) is quite meaningless for estimating the income to be generated from a purchase, because the price at which the share or stock stands in the market may be very different from the nominal value; it may be higher, it may be lower. If the £1 shares are worth only 33p the 4p (or 4%) net dividend would be the net income on a capital outlay of 33p, equivalent to a net return of 12.12%. To express it as a yield this figure would need to be grossed up for tax. Assuming a basic rate of 30% tax, a figure of 12.12% net represents a gross yield of 17.3%.

Assessing ordinary shares

Deciding whether to buy or sell the shares of any particular company or shares in any particular sector of the economy is really an exercise in forecasting what is going to happen in the future to that company or in that industry. Will it expand or contract? Will the company be well managed, enjoying the benefits of new inventions, or will it suffer from technical obsolescence of plant?

Professional investors and others with specialist knowledge have the time and ability to make careful analyses of the conditions in which whole industries and companies within them operate. The amateur investor can only seek advice and supplement that advice by the application of a few elementary tests based on the figures in the company's published accounts.

Balance sheets

Companies whose shares are officially quoted on the Stock

Personal investment

Exchange have to publish full accounts at the end of their trading year, and an interim report halfway through the year. How to read a company balance sheet is discussed in Chapter 14. Here we shall outline some of the facts that a would-be buyer of shares can learn from the published accounts. A specimen simplified balance sheet and profit and loss account appears opposite.

It is customary for a company's assets to be listed on the right-hand side of the balance sheet, and the liabilities on the left. One of the liabilities will be the nominal value of the issued ordinary shares, and another will be the 'reserve', which is the total of the accumulated undistributed profits over the past years. If these two figures are added together you have a figure for what is often described as 'ordinary shareholders' funds'.

Assets value

If you now deduct from the figure of ordinary shareholders' funds the total balance sheet value of those assets that may have no saleable value – such as 'Preliminary Expenses', 'Goodwill' or 'Loss on Profit and Loss Account', which may be thought of as fictitious assets – and divide the resultant figure by the number of ordinary shares in issue, you arrive at a figure for 'value of assets per share'. You are now in a position to compare the market price of the share with its net asset value, but unless you are an expert investment analyst you may not be able to draw any safe conclusions from any disparity between the two figures without exhaustive research into the reasons for it. People don't buy shares just because of their asset value, but for their potential income and growth.

Profit and loss account

With the balance sheet there will be a profit and loss account. The accounts of many public companies do not show all the details of how the profit figure is arrived at, but they do show turnover (total sales), and usually the direct operating costs together with all the remaining expenses in total. Net profit before tax is always shown. One can take a view on the ability of the company to continue paying dividends at the current rate, or to increase that rate, by comparing total net after-tax profits available for ordinary shareholders with total dividend. If profits are being retained in the company there is a prospect for growth, providing that adequate provision is being made for maintaining the real value of the company.

DEF LTD
Simplified Balance Sheet

Liabilities	£	£	Assets	£	£
Shareholders' funds			*Fixed*		
Issued share capital of 500,000 ordinary 50p shares		250,000	Premises and machinery		310,000
Reserves		225,000	Patents		61,000
		475,000			371,000
Long-term liabilities			*Current assets*		
Bank loan	100,000		Stocks of		
Provision for tax	51,000	151,000	material	172,000	
Current liabilities			Stocks of goods	53,000	
Sundry creditors		25,000	Sundry debtors	20,000	
			Cash at bank	35,000	280,000
		651,000			651,000

Profit and Loss Appropriation Account

	£
Net profit before tax	108,500
Provision for tax	51,000
Net profit after tax	57,500
Dividend paid	37,500
Transfer to Reserve	20,000
	57,500

Price/earnings ratio

Some of the ratios of balance sheet and profit and loss figures are published as a matter of routine in the financial press – for of course it is the ratios between certain figures in the accounts that are significant for investors, rather than merely the absolute size of such figures. For example, each Saturday the better newspapers quote for each share, as well as the closing market price, the dividend yield (percentage of gross dividend to share price), and also the number of times the dividend actually paid over the last year can be divided into the profits *available* for that dividend. This ratio is called 'times covered'.

Example

AB Company Ltd has an issued capital of 200,000 ordinary £1 shares. These are priced in the market at 130p. Last year's total after-tax net profit came to £35,000, and a dividend of 7p net per share was paid, 3p as interim and 4p as final. A net dividend of 7p is equivalent to a gross dividend of 10p before tax at 30%.

So yield is:

$$\frac{10}{130} = 7.69\%$$

And net earnings per share were:

$$\frac{35,000}{200,000} = 17\frac{1}{2}p$$

So dividend was covered 2½ times $\quad \frac{17\frac{1}{2}}{7}$

A high dividend cover indicates large retention of profits and suggests the company may be expanding or poised to expand. Prospects for future rises in dividend and price of shares appear, on the face of things, good. On the other hand, high dividend cover may merely indicate that the fairly recent removal of government restrictions on dividend increase may not yet have worked through. It does not do to make snap judgements without looking behind the figures to the realities.

When total attributable profits are divided by the number of shares in issue one arrives at a figure for earnings per share. If earnings per share are then related to share price one arrives at another useful indicator, the price/earnings ratio (P/E ratio). In the above example, with a share price of 130 and net earnings per share of 17½p, the P/E ratio was:

$$\frac{130}{17.5} = 7.4$$

That means that the share is priced at 7.4 times the annual profits earned per share. The lower the P/E ratio the poorer is the market's assessment of the share as a potential earner of income and growth. Of course, the market may be wrong.

Example

The following is the profit and loss appropriation account of a company whose issued share capital consists of 100,000 £1 10% preference shares and two million 25p ordinary shares, which are priced at 42p on the market.

	£	£
Net profit before tax		522,500
Corporation tax		258,600
Net profit after tax		263,900
Dividend on preference shares (net)		7,000
		256,900
Interim ordinary dividend	29,400 (net)	
Proposed final dividend	74,400 (net)	103,800 (=£148,285
Transfer to Reserve account		gross)
		153,100
		256,900

It will be seen that the preference shareholders must be paid their dividend out of taxed profits before the amount of profit earned for ordinary shareholders is arrived at. So earned for ordinaries is £256,900, not £263,900.

Earnings per share $\dfrac{256,900}{2,000,000}$ = 12.845p net

Total dividend per share $\dfrac{103,800}{2,000,000}$ = 5.19p net

Dividend yield $\dfrac{5.19 \times 100}{42}$ = 12.35% net (=17.65% gross)

P/E ratio $\dfrac{42}{12.845}$ = 3.27

The shares appear to be underpriced.

Inflation accounting

The persistently high level of inflation in recent years has brought to the fore the inadequacies of traditional methods of accounting, under which, of course, the calculation of profits has been based on the historic costs of producing the output sold. It is now being recognised that for a company to be seen from its accounts to have earned profits of £100,000, in a year during which the cost of replacing its obsolescing fixed assets has risen by £100,000 more than the amount charged in the accounts for depreciation of assets, really means that it has made no profits.

Or again, a small distributing business that bought goods for resale on the first day of its operation for £60,000, and sold them all on the last day of its first year for £90,000, would, under historic costs accounting, show a gross trading profit of £30,000. But if prices rose during the year by 20% it will cost the business £72,000 to replace its stock to enable it to continue trading on the same scale. The real profits are thus not £30,000 but £18,000.

Attempts to overcome this problem include the proposed introduction of new methods of accounting, of which the most widely accepted version appears to be Current Cost Accounting. This method seeks to revalue each asset at the end of each year at its current replacement cost rather than its historic cost. The effect on different companies, and on companies in different industries, of adopting CCA will vary very greatly, and the practical value to share analysts of the concepts of earnings-per-share and price/earnings ratios may well disappear, since the definition of 'earnings' will no longer be on a common basis.

Growth and inflation

The average rewards in the way of current dividends being comparatively low on ordinary shares, one would expect to find that the value of shareholdings would be rising – otherwise why should people be willing to buy them? Of course, some shares *have* risen substantially, but the average movement in market prices between 1974 and 1980 has been only just sufficient for them to have retained their real value. The so-called growth element has been completely absent.

Several index numbers are compiled daily and published to indicate the general movement in prices. The best known of these indices is the *Financial Times* Index of Industrial Ordinary Shares (the FT Index) based on 30 of the leading large company shares in the industrial sector. Another one is the FT All-share Index, which is accepted as a better representative guide to movements in share prices generally.

In Fig. 6.1 the movements from 1970 to 1980 in the FT All-share Index are plotted against the movements in the Retail Price Index (the value of money). Over the period the average money value of shares has risen from 135 to 248, an apparent growth of 84%. But over the same period the RPI has climbed from 75 to 252, indicating that money in 1980 was worth less than a third of its value in 1970. So the 1980 share index of 248, if it were to be adjusted for inflation, should be divided by 3.3, making it around 75. This indicates that people who have held shares since 1970 have, on average, lost half the value of their capital in real terms.

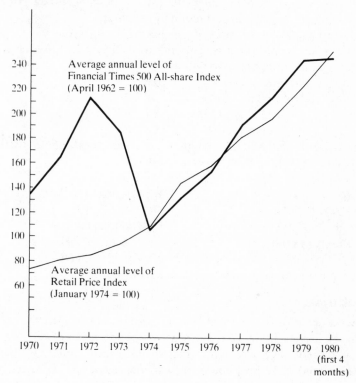

Fig. 6.1

Three further dramatic conclusions can be drawn from the graph. First, people who bought shares in 1970 and sold out in the heady days of 1972, made a good profit both in money terms and in real terms. Second, those who bought in 1972 and sold in 1974 lost half their capital in two years. Third, people who bought in the recession of 1974, and were still holding the shares in 1980, saw their holdings just keep pace with inflation; but there was no real growth.

Dealing costs

For buying or selling ordinary shares on the Stock Exchange you have to use the services of a stockbroker. You may either instruct a stockbroker direct, or you can ask your bank or your solicitor to handle the transaction for you, in which case the bank's or solicitor's own stockbroker will act. The following gives an idea of what the costs are likely to be:

Transfer stamp. A government tax of 2% of the contract price has to be paid by the buyer, but not by the seller.

Contract stamp. A contract stamp has to be affixed to the copy of the contract note that is sent both to the buyer and the seller. These are the rates of stamp duty:

bargains of £100 or less	free
bargains from £100 to £500	10p
£500 to £1,500	30p
over £1,500	60p

Brokerage. The official minimum scale of stockbroking commission, payable by both buyer and seller, is:

£200 or less	at discretion of broker
£200 to £467	£7
£467 to £7,000	1.5% of total bargain
£7,000 to £100,000	1.5% on first £7000, plus 0.5% on remainder

Commission on larger amounts is at a reducing rate.

Unit trusts

Investing directly in the purchase of company stocks and shares carries more risk, both as to income and growth, than many small investors are willing to undertake. But they, and others who lack the knowledge, experience, or skill adequately to supervise their shareholdings, can participate indirectly in the stock and share market by buying units of unit trusts.

A unit trust is a fund invested in a large range of undertakings, ordinary company shares, overseas shares, preference shares, and so on. Each unit holder thus enjoys a wide spread of risk since he has only a very small interst in a very large number of different companies.

Units are easy to buy and sell, but it has to be realised that prices can go down as well as up, as unit prices are determined by the market prices of the underlying portfolio of investments. Although unit trusts must be considered essentially speculative, the risk is so spread that price movements are slower and smaller than those of shares.

Historically, and over the long term, most unit trusts have risen considerably in value, as well as paying out regular distributions of income earned on the underlying investments. Different trusts offer different mixes of shares, so that there is a wide range of trusts to choose from. Some are geared particularly for capital growth, some for high income and lower growth. The better-managed unit trusts have far outpaced the FT Index.

Units in many trusts can be purchased by a regular monthly savings plan. You give your bank a standing order and units are bought for you each month in the trust you select. A variation, and a very profitable one, is to link the savings plan to life assurance. By this device you can take advantage of the tax relief accorded to premiums on 'qualifying' life assurance policies (*see* Chapter 12).

Instead of your monthly contribution being used directly to buy trust units, it is treated as a premium on a life assurance policy on your life. The policy is linked to the unit trust and practically all the contributions, except those for the first few months, are invested in units. Because each contribution is legally a 'premium' on a life assurance policy, the actual amount you pay to the trust managers is deemed to be 'net of tax relief at 17.5%' (15% from April 1981). That means that the managers can claim a further amount from the Inland Revenue. Consequently each £82.50 contribution you make is worth £100 of unit trust units.

This is really a long-term investment and ought to be kept going for at least four years or more. You can surrender any time you like, but a surrender within ten years involves some small penalties.

Life assurance as investment

The subject of life assurance generally is treated in Chapter 12. A particular form of life assurance policy called an 'endowment policy' is described in some detail on page 135. This kind of policy sets up a capital sum which becomes payable to you at the end of the agreed endowment period as well as providing protection for your dependants.

The possibility of using endowment policies as a savings and investment medium should not be overlooked in any long-term plan. The tax-free yield on the regular premiums invested can work out as high as 10.5% per annum.

TEST QUESTIONS

1. What are ordinary shares in a limited comapny?
2. Why are ordinary shares sometimes called 'equities'?
3. Explain the divergence between market value and nominal value of ordinary shares.
4. How can companies acquire additional capital for expansion from their own resources?
5. It is said that the market price of a share is not determined by the value of the company's net assets. Why is this so? What *does* determine market price?
6. How is the yield on an ordinary share calculated?
7. If dividend yield on shares is below current interest rates, what can a potential buyer of the shares be expecting to gain from a purchase of the shares?
8. Is income tax payable on dividends received?
9. What is a 'tax credit'?
10. Describe one of two ways in which the asset value of a share can be assessed in a rough and ready way from balance sheet figures.
11. What is meant by 'number of times covered' in the case of the dividend on ordinary shares?
12. What is the significance of the price/earnings ratio of shares?
13. Describe a unit trust.
14. What advantages do unit trusts have over direct purchases of individual company shares?
15. What kind of life assurance policies can be a profitable means of long-term investment for the regular saver?

EXERCISES

A   Calculate from the accounts of DEF Ltd printed on page 67 the following indicators, assuming the share price of the 50p shares to be 82p:

Yield on ordinaries
Times dividend covered
P/E ratio.

B   You decide to buy 1,000 ordinary 50p shares in the same company, DEF Ltd. If your broker quotes you 80½p per share, what will the purchase cost you, including all charges?

PART THREE

Sources and costs of personal finance

7 Finance and credit facilities

Most of the expenditure of the private individual is financed out of his current income – which is another way of saying that what he buys he pays for in cash out of wages or salary. But for most people there are occasions when they need to buy some major item, the price of which is more than can be found in cash at once. In order to acquire the item extra finance is needed. In this chapter we shall review various methods of financing expenditure other than out of current income or from money already saved up.

Buying on credit

In the wholesale trade few sales are for cash. Most take place on credit. A shopkeeper buying goods from a manufacturer will receive a bill each month or quarter for what has been delivered to him the previous month or months. He will settle this with one cheque. Where retail turnover is rapid, as with food shops, the retailer is often paid for his sales before he has himself paid for the purchases, which gives him a supply of free credit!

In former days it was also quite usual for retail domestic purchases to be made 'on credit account'. One would order groceries, meat, vegetables and so on, no payment being made at the time of delivery, the cost being entered instead on an account kept by the supplier who would send his bill at the end of the month. This would usually be paid within a few days of receiving it. Often the bill would be marked '5% discount for payment within seven days', which encouraged prompt payment.

Now that most retail purchases of food are made in supermarkets this practice has almost disappeared. It lingers on in the case of milk deliveries, where a week's credit is usually taken, and newspaper deliveries, where the credit period is usually a month. Discount for prompt payment of these small items has also been abandoned.

It will be obvious that since the shopkeeper who does not insist on cash payment needs more liquid capital to finance his trade than a cash trader will need, his total operating costs are going to be higher. His customers should expect the extra cost (interest on extra capital needed) to be passed on to them in higher prices. It is indeed quite normal to find that cash prices in 'no credit' shops are significantly lower than in the old-fashioned family grocer.

Interest-free credit

Although buying food on a credit account has practically disappeared, buying household goods like clothing or consumer durables on credit has increased very considerably. The simplest credit purchase is one where the seller sets a retail price for an article and offers to accept, say, a 20% deposit and the balance in equal monthly instalments – often nine instalments – no interest or other charge being made. If the retail price were £100 the deposit would be £20 followed by nine payments each of £8.89.

As with the old-fashioned family grocer giving interest-free credit, a shopkeeper offering deferred terms without making any charge for them must be pricing his goods at a high enough level to cover the interest he will have to pay on the extra capital employed (if he is having to borrow the capital), or the interest he is forfeiting on capital (if he is using his own resources). A would-be cash purchaser at such a shop would reasonably expect to be able to obtain a discount off the marked retail price. But he will have to ask for it; a shop offering interest-free credit is unlikely at the same time openly to admit that the goods would have been cheaper if the buyer were not to take credit, for to do so would belie the offer of 'free' credit.

How much discount?

To determine what a reasonable discount rate would be, one can work out what the credit being offered free is actually costing the supplier. If the cost of money is, say, 10% per annum, a customer taking £80 credit repayable in nine monthly instalments is, in effect, borrowing £80 for one month, £71.11 for two months, and so on. He is borrowing less and less as the nine months pass. If it were to be mathematically calculated, the interest element would effectively be the interest for nine months on approximately half the original amount borrowed. Interest at 10% on £40 over nine months is £3. So a £3 discount for cash (nearly 4%) would be an appropriate rate. If a shop will not agree to giving discount for cash the purchaser will very likely find he can buy the item £3 cheaper from another establishment not offering free credit.

Advantages of discount

The following advantages could accrue to a trader giving discount:

(*a*)   economy in use of capital, having less tied up in 'sundry debtors';

(*b*)   increase in sales, although profit per unit is smaller;

(*c*)   no need to keep complex book-keeping records of credit sales and amounts outstanding.

Credit cards

Using a consumer credit card such as Access or Barclaycard is very similar in its consequences to buying on simple credit. With a credit card you purchase the article at the marked retail price, but instead of paying for it there and then you present your card and sign a special sales voucher. All your purchases during a month are billed to you by the credit card company the following month. If you pay within 25 days of the date of the statement you are, in effect, getting free credit for a short period. If you prefer to take extended credit you can pay off the amount in monthly instalments of not less than 5% of the outstanding balance. But in that case you pay interest. In 1980 the interest rate was 2.25% per month on the outstanding balance. This works out at a true interest rate of up to 30.6% per annum.

You pay nothing for the use of Access or Barclaycard. And if you don't take extended credit you can take up to around a month's credit without any charge at all. So who is paying the cost of all this? The answer is the retailer. He receives payment for his sales from the credit card company; however, he doesn't get the full retail price of the goods that *you* are having to pay, but an amount lower than the retail price by a percentage agreed by the retailer and the credit card company. In effect, therefore, the retailer is giving discount not to you, the purchaser, but to the credit card company. This discount provides the credit card company with funds with which to meet the costs of its operations.

It follows from this that any shop offering to accept a credit card ought also to offer, as an alternative, a discount for immediate cash payment. But not many shops do this.

Instalment credit

Apart from the use of general credit cards such as Access or Barclaycard there are three other main ways of obtaining instalment credit for the purchase of merchandise. It is important to distinguish between the different methods for not only may the respective costs be different in each case, but the legal position of the customer *vis-a-vis* the seller may be different.

By an order made under the Consumer Credit Act 1974 it has been illegal since October 1980 for anybody offering consumer credit not to provide certain minimum information to the customer. In particular the offerer of credit must quote the true annual interest rate and the total cost of the credit including any charges, and the amount of each instalment and the number and frequency of the instalments. In this way every offer of credit can be compared as to its costs with any other form of credit.

Charge card

The charge card is the modern equivalent of the old-fashioned monthly credit account. It is now generally called a charging account and is operated by many of the big department stores. In essence the system is very similar to that of Access or Barclaycard. The shop provides the customer with a charge card (after having checked the customer's credit status) and this card can be used *in that shop only* almost exactly as with Access or Barclaycard. The customer gets about a month's free credit; for extended credit repayable by monthly instalments he pays interest. Rates of interest ranged in 1980 from 1.75% to 2.5% per month on the outstanding balance, so the true rate of interest lay between 25.3% and 30.6% per annum. You are generally required to make a minimum monthly payment of 5% of the balance or £5, whichever is the higher.

Example

	£
Total purchases in month (Minimum payment to be made within the stipulated period is £10.)	200
Balance brought forward	200
First monthly payment	30
Balance outstanding	170
add Interest at 2%	3.40
Balance	173.40

(The next minimum monthly payment will be £8.67, being 5% of £173.40.)

A person buying goods by this method becomes the owner of the goods as soon as he obtains possession.

Credit sale

The second method of obtaining instalment credit is slightly less flexible than a charge account in that the period of repayment and the monthly instalment are both fixed at the outset. It is thus what might be called a 'structured loan' in that the structure of the complete transaction is predetermined. The usual name for this arrangement is 'credit sale'. The interest charge is lower than for extended credit under a charge account.

Under a credit sale agreement a purchaser agrees to pay a cash deposit at the time of purchase. The deposit required ranges upwards from 10% depending on the type of goods. For many items the minimum down payment is fixed by law. The customer also agrees to repay the balance plus interest over a selected period of up to three years or so. Interest at a stated percentage flat rate (in 1980 it was commonly 12.5% or 13.5% per annum) of the original debt for the whole of the selected period is added to the debt at the outset. This total is divided by the number of months in the credit period to give the monthly repayment instalment required.

Example

In one transaction a customer agrees to buy several items of furniture.

	£
Total retail price	400
Deposit required 10%	40
Original debt (carried over)	360

	£
Original debt (brought forward)	360
Interest charged at 13.5% per annum over 24 months on original debt	98
Balance to be paid by 24 monthly instalments of £19.09	458
Total credit price	498

True rate of interest is 26.8% per annum.

Under a credit sale the purchaser becomes the owner of the goods outright as soon as he signs the contract. Should he default on his repayments the whole of the outstanding debt becomes payable and he can be sued for that amount.

Most department stores and some other large retailers now finance their own instalment credit plans, but the majority of smaller distributors arrange the credit through one of the finance companies.

Flat rate and true rate

Notice particularly that the quoted rate of interest is a flat rate, by which is meant that it is calculated on the original amount borrowed for the whole of the credit period. But since the purchaser is repaying part of his borrowing each month he is in effect paying interest on money he is not borrowing! Indeed, a flat rate over one or two years works out at a true rate of about twice the flat rate. The true annual percentage rate of interest under a credit sale agreement ranged in 1980 from 24% to 27%. Rates vary, of course, from shop to shop.

Hire purchase

Buying on hire purchase is very similar to buying on credit sale agreement. But there is one important difference. When an article is acquired on HP the legal contract that the customer makes with the supplier is that the customer will *hire* the item for the duration of the contract, paying a 'rental' for its use, and will have the option to purchase it for a nominal sum at the end of the period. There is thus a legal distinction between a hire-purchase contract and any other form of instalment purchase, for under HP the goods remain the property of the supplier until the final payment is made. Until that moment the supplier has certain rights of regaining possession of the goods should instalments fall into arrears (although the purchaser now has valuable legal safeguards that need not be gone into here).

Personal finance

Under any other form of credit the supplier has no rights of repossessing the goods. He can, of course, sue on the debt.

Example

	£
Retail price of goods	249
Deposit paid	49
Balance outstanding	200
Interest charge at 19.5% per annum for one year	39
Balance to be paid in 12 monthly instalments of £19.92	239
Total credit price (£249 + £39)	288

The true rate of interest in this case works out at about 38% per annum. This is unusually high and a better deal could probably be obtained by shopping around.

Budget account

Many shops, particularly outfitters and drapers, offer a budget facility. This is designed for financing not a single purchase of a high-priced article, but for repeated small purchases. The customer decides how much he can afford to pay the shop as a monthly instalment (a minimum payment is usually set of £2 to £5), and the shop allows him to purchase goods to the value of, say, 24 times the instalment.

This is a useful device from the trader's point of view since it encourages the customer to deal regularly with him; and from the customer's angle it affords the useful facility of 'revolving credit', for he can continue taking fresh credit as he pays off the old – provided only that the outstanding debt may never exceed the stated number of monthly instalments.

Interest is charged monthly on the amount outstanding at the same rate as is charged for extended credit on a charge account, so that the true interest cost is again around 25% to 30% per annum.

Comparative costs

All purchases made under any form of credit arrangement are virtually a borrowing of money. Of the methods so far outlined different purchasers may find that some one method has special features that happen to suit their purposes. Nevertheless, one should be aware that there can be quite a wide disparity in costs.

Type of credit	Range of true interest rates per annum (1980)
Interest-free credit	Nil (or discount forfeited)
Credit cards	Nil for about one month; around 30.6% for extended credit
Charge account	Approximately as for credit cards
Credit sale	26.8% to over 32%
Shop's budget account	About 25% to 30%
Hire purchase	Varies up to 38%

These are only sample rates obtained from different suppliers. Hire purchase is seldom used nowadays except for car purchases, where it is usually the only method by which a finance company will provide finance. Since the risk of loss is higher in this field than in other fields, the true rates tend to be higher. In some cases it could cost a true rate of up to 45% to purchase an old second-hand car on HP.

Other sources of credit

To accept the first form of credit that is offered by a supplier of goods is unwise without first checking that the cost of that credit is reasonable as compared with other sources of credit. In many cases it may be more economical to obtain a loan in money and to pay cash for your purchases. Advantage can then sometimes be taken of any cash discounts available, and in the case of expenditure on such things as road fund licences and rail season tickets you can often save more money over a year by taking an annual contract instead of a daily or weekly one, than it costs in borrowing the money for the purpose.

Example

	Annual outlay £
Daily rail fare from A to B is £1.74 (assume 5 days per week for 49 weeks less 1 bank holiday per month)	407.16
Weekly ticket costs £7.40 for 49 weeks	362.60
Monthly contract costs £28.40 × 12 (but £21 is saved by omitting the month of holiday and taking a weekly ticket for the odd week)	319.80
Quarterly contract costs £81.80 × 4	327.20

Annual contract costs	294.00
Personal bank loan for £294 at 11% flat for 1 year	
	326.28

Purchasing an annual contract with a personal loan is therefore cheaper than a daily ticket, a weekly ticket, or a quarterly contract, though not cheaper than a monthly ticket, modified for the annual three-week holiday.

Bank finance

For an established bank customer of impeccable credit rating, a personal loan from his bank is usually a cheaper way of financing the purchase of a high-priced consumer durable than any of the forms of credit discussed in the earlier sections of this chapter.

A personal bank loan is a structured loan, on similar lines to the structure of any form of instalment credit. A personal loan may be arranged for any amount from £50 upwards and for any period up to five years. If the loan is required for the purchase of any item which, were it otherwise being acquired by hire purchase, would have been subject to a statutory minimum down payment, then the bank will expect the amount of the loan not to exceed the cost price less the down payment.

Interest is fixed for the whole period of the borrowing and is added to the amount of the loan at the outset. Flat rate of interest in early 1980 was usually 11% per annum on the amount borrowed, which makes the effective true rate range from 20.2% to 21.8%, depending on the precise period of repayment.

Example

	£
Cost of goods	400
Cash loan required	360
Interest at 11% for 24 months	79.20
To be repaid in 24 monthly instalments of £18.30	439.20
True interest rate is 21.7% per annum	

Had this been financed by credit sale (*see* page 80) the instalment would have been £19.05 instead of £18.30, and the true interest rate would have been 26.63%.

A bank is willing to grant a personal loan to a creditworthy customer for any purpose, provided only that the bank is satisfied that the facility is in the customer's own interests and is not facilitating his living beyond his means. For instance, holidays, car purchase, repairs to the roof of your house can all be financed by personal loan.

For occasional needs for short-term credit a bank might be willing to grant an overdraft facility, which is often easier and more flexible than a personal loan. It is suitable only for meeting the unexpected contingencies that beset us all from time to time when a particularly large unplanned expenditure has to be met.

An overdraft is a drawing out from your current account of sums of money in excess of what there is in it. In appropriate circumstances a bank manager may allow a customer to overdraw up to a stated limit and for a brief period of months, but the bank's agreement *must* be obtained beforehand. Cheques issued in excess of the credit balance may be returned unpaid if no arrangement for an overdraft has been agreed to.

Interest rate on overdrafts is always a fluctuating one, between 2% and 5% above current base rate. When base rate changes so does overdraft rate, the margin remaining the same. Interest is worked out on the daily balance, so with an overdraft the quoted interest rate is identical with the true rate of interest.

Bank budget accounts

Two of the big banks offer a budget account facility to customers. This should not be confused with a shop budget account, although the principles are very similar. With a bank budget account the customer has to make a detailed estimate of all the big items of household expenditure he expects to have to pay over a 12-month period, and add them together. Each month a sum representing one-twelfth of the total annual expenditure is transferred from the ordinary current account to a special budget account opened in the customer's name. He will be given a separate cheque book for use on this account and each time he has to pay a bill catered for under his budget plan he pays it from the budget account.

This effectively spreads the otherwise uneven load of large bills smoothly throughout the year. Sometimes the budget account will go overdrawn (in debit). That is what it is intended for. But at the end of the year it should be just about all square. Interest is charged on any borrowing at a margin above base rate. With base rate at 16% in 1980 the interest rate on budget accounts was 20%. This is also the true rate.

Paying bills by instalment

Electricity and gas boards offer facilities for paying their bills in monthly instalments, usually by banker's order. The most popular of these methods consists of the consumer's making payments each month for a year, the amounts being based on the consumption of gas or electricity *in the preceding twelve months*. There is neither loss nor gain in the cost to the consumer, for if his consumption goes up or down in any year, then the final payment is adjusted to take this into account. There are no interest payments, for no credit is being given.

Insurance companies

Another possible source of finance is available to anybody who has a life assurance policy on which he has been paying premiums for a number of years. Endowment policies and whole-life policies (*see* Chapter 12 on insurance) acquire a 'surrender value' after a certain period. The surrender value is the amount of cash that the insurance company is prepared to pay to the holder in exchange for cancelling the whole of the insurance contract. No further premiums would be payable on the policy and no further benefits could arise on it.

Commonly the surrender value of a policy that has been running for seven or eight years or less will be lower than the actual net cost of the premiums on it to date. After ten years the surrender value will usually be significantly higher than the cost of the premiums – especially will this be the case if the policy was a 'with-profits' one (*see* Chapter 12).

As an alternative to surrendering a policy for cash it is usually possible to obtain a loan from the insurance company itself on the security of the policy. The amount of the loan will be restricted to the current surrender value. The interest rate charged is usually rather lower than on a loan from other sources because the insurance company derives more revenue from a policy holder who continues to pay premiums (although taking a loan on the policy) than from one who surrenders for cash and ceases to pay premiums.

Notional abatement of cost of loans

Inflation

When assessing the pros and cons of seeking finance for an immediate purchase as compared with deferring that purchase until you have saved up enough money to pay cash for it, you should not only compare the costs of the various methods of finance, but also the possible costs of deferring purchase. In other words, you should consider the likely course of inflation – the probable rise in price of the article to be bought between the present time and the time when cash resources will be sufficient, abated by any interest earned on cash currently saved. You should also allow for the probable rise in your money income during the period of deferment.

For instance, if hi-fi equipment priced today at £249 were to rise in price to £286 in one year's time, it might be argued that it is better business to acquire it immediately on hire purchase at a total eventual hire-purchase cost of £288, since to do so would give you a year's use of the equipment for only £2.

It could also be argued that were the price of the equipment to rise by only 11% in the year to £276.50, it would still pay to buy it today using the finance of a personal bank loan at a flat interest rate of 11%.

In times of inflation it should also be borne in mind that, provided income rises in line with inflation, the real burden of making the contractual fixed repayment instalments becomes less as time passes, since each instalment represents a smaller fraction of income. In inflationary conditions borrowers make a gain, while lenders of money make a loss.

Tax relief

A private individual who pays interest on any form of finance for the purpose of enabling him to buy his own home, to extend it, or to improve it, is entitled to tax relief at his top rate of income tax on the interest paid each year. Relief is restricted to interest on a total borrowing of £25,000. This rule applies whatever the source of finance and is not confined to borrowing from building societies.

Thus a bank customer who obtains a personal loan of £800 for the purpose of installing central heating in his home, on which he has a building society mortgage of not more than £24,000, will find that the real cost to him after tax relief of paying the true rate of interest of 20.6% per annum will be only seven-tenths of this, namely 14.42%, if he is a basic-rate tax-payer.

No tax relief is available on any kind of borrowing for purposes other than those mentioned above.

TEST QUESTIONS

1. Name six methods of obtaining credit for the purchase of consumer durable goods.
2. In what circumstances would it be reasonable to expect a discount for cash on a retail purchase?
3. Based on the flat interest rate quoted for credit repayable by equal monthly instalments, describe a formula for calculating the approximate true rate of interest payable.
4. Give two examples of methods for obtaining one month's free credit on shop purchases.
5. Who bears the cost of 'free' credit available with a credit card?
6. What is meant by a 'structured' loan?
7. Describe a credit sale agreement.
8. Distinguish between a credit sale agreement and a hire-purchase agreement.
9. How does a shop budget account work?
10. It is claimed that for extended credit on a credit card you would be charged interest at a higher true rate than that on hire-purchase or credit sale, because greater flexibility is repaying the credit is provided. Explain this.
11. Distinguish between a bank overdraft and a personal loan.
12. How is the interest rate determined on an overdraft?
13. Explain the purpose of a bank budget account.
14. In what circumstances can a loan be obtained from an insurance company?
15. In what sense might it be cheaper to buy now on credit terms than to save up and pay cash later on?
16. Is tax relief available on interest paid on borrowed money?

EXERCISES

A Jill Anscombe decides to purchase electrical equipment priced at £250. She has insufficient money saved to pay cash and discovers the following alternative methods of financing the purchase:

(a) The shop offers hire-purchase terms of 20% deposit with the balance payable over 30 months in monthly instalments. The total credit price is £312.50.

(b) Alternatively the shop offers credit sale terms of £50 deposit followed by 30 monthly instalments of £8.92.

(c)   Her bank is willing to give Jill a personal loan for the purpose over two years. It will lend £200 at a flat interest rate of 11% per annum.

Which method provides the lowest total cost? And which method entails the lowest outlay per month?

B   Bob Carruthers opens a budget account at an outfitters. He pays £10 immediately and agrees to pay a monthly instalment of £10, which gives him revolving credit of up to £240. Interest at 2% per month will be added to the outstanding debt each month. In the first month he buys goods priced at £83, and in the second month further goods priced at £44. Calculate the outstanding debt at the end of two months when Bob will have paid a total of £30.

8 Mortgages

For the purchase of a house almost everybody needs finance by way of what is called a mortgage loan. This is secured by a legal charge, or 'mortgage', on the property. It is possible to obtain mortgage loans from many sources in certain conditions – private investors, local authorities, insurance companies, and banks – but the vast majority of mortgage loans on residential property are provided by building societies.

Building societies give priority for the allocation of their limited supply of funds to their existing members. During 1979 and 1980 some societies were restricting the granting of new mortgages to members who had been saving with them regularly for at least two years, and had in their account at least 10% of the purchase price of the property. Anybody contemplating needing a mortgage should, therefore, take early steps to become a building society saver.

Amount of mortgage

Proportion of value

Normally a building society will limit the amount it is prepared to lend on a property to 95% of the purchase price or of the society's own valuation if this is lower. For purchases under £14,000 a loan of 100% is not impossible from some societies, but in times of high interest rates and shortage of mortgage funds, loans of this proportion are unlikely. A purchaser would be wise to expect to have to put up at least 10% of the purchase price in cash from his own resources. This amount happens to coincide with the amount that a purchaser will have to pay as cash deposit on signing the legal contract for the purchase.

Multiple of income

The maximum loan will also be restricted by the size of the prospective borrower's income. The purpose of this is to ensure that the paying of the interest and repayment instalments on the loan will be within the capacity of the borrower.

Societies have different formulae for this purpose but all base the formula on a multiple of income. A good rule of thumb is that the total lending will be restricted to two to two and a half times the applicant's annual gross income. For this purpose income may be taken to mean basic earnings plus *guaranteed* weighting allowances, *guaranteed* commission or bonus, and *guaranteed* overtime. Where the extra earnings are usual but not guaranteed, a half of their total may be added to the basic earnings figure.

In the case of a joint mortgage of husband and wife the formula is usually two to two and a half times the larger income plus once the smaller.

Example

Rupert and Mary Stott earn gross incomes of £6,000 and £4,000 respectively. They have £4,500 saved up in a building society share account and wish to buy a purpose-built flat for £23,000. The society's valuer places a figure of £22,000 only on it.

Maximum loan restricted to 90% of valuation = £19,800
Maximum loan restricted by income:

$$2\frac{1}{2} \times £6,000 = £15,000$$
$$1 \times £4,000 = \underline{4,000} \qquad \underline{£19,000}$$

Thus £19,000 is the maximum loan. This will require the couple to find £4,000 from their own resources, plus a few hundreds for their expenses. Although they have more than £4,000 in their investment account this is barely sufficient to cover also the initial costs of buying. They might consider using the society's low valuation as a lever for getting a reduction in the price.

In times of very high interest rates such as those prevailing during 1980, the formula may be modified to twice the major income plus half the minor income, to ensure that the borrowers would not be overcommitting themselves with the larger outgoings. As a general guide a society will be unwilling for the repayments on a mortgage to exceed one quarter of the major income.

Indemnity guarantee

The rules of most societies require additional security to be taken for any loan that exceeds a stated proportion, often 80% of the valuation of the property. The additional security usually takes the form of an independent guarantee from an insurance company indemnifying the society against loss in respect of the excess lending over 80%.

The cost of this indemnity has to be met by the borrower, but it is quite modest and is in the form of a single premium, the amount of which can usually be added to the mortgage amount so that it, too, is being borrowed from the society.

The single premium is commonly at a rate between 3% and 4.5% of the excess borrowing. So if the society is lending £18,000, being 90% of the valuation of £20,000, then the excess lending is 10% of £20,000, which is £2,000. Single premium at 3.5% would be £70.

Mortgage period

Building society mortgages are normally arranged in such a way that they will be repaid over an agreed period of years. It is sometimes possible to arrange for a 30-year mortgage but 25 years is more normal. A shorter term may be requested by the borrower, but the shorter the period of years the larger the monthly outgoing will be. In times of inflation it is good business to borrow money over a long period and to repay it from devalued pounds out of a continually increasing money income.

Mortgage interest

The interest rate charged on a building society mortgage is a variable one, not fixed as with a bank personal loan, for instance. This means that the rate can be lowered or raised during the term of the mortgage. The rate has to be variable because the rates of interest allowed to society investors are variable. Both rates have to change from time to time to keep them broadly in line with the general level of interest rates in the market.

Setting the rate

Most societies adopt for their basic mortgage rate the rate recommended by the Building Societies Association. But societies are free to charge a lower or higher rate if they choose to do so. Some societies make a practice of charging a rate marginally higher than the recommended rate because they also pay investors a marginally higher rate.

Differential rates

It is now common practice for building societies to charge mortgage interest at what are called 'differential' interest rates, by which is meant that a higher rate is charged for a large mortgage than for a small. Mortgages up to a certain limit are charged at the recommended rate, but progressively larger mortages are charged at progressively higher rates. Two specimen scales are shown below, based on a recommended mortgage rate of 12%.

	Society A	Society B
Loans up to £13,000		12%
Loans up to £14,999	12%	
£13,001 to £15,000		12.5%
£15,001 to £17,000		12.5%
£15,000 to £19,999	12.5%	
£17,001 to £19,000		12.75%
Over £19,999	13%	
£19,001 to £21,000		13%
£21,001 to £25,000		13.25%
Over £25,000		13.5%

Where a differential rate of interest is charged the higher rate applies to the whole of the loan, not just to the successive slices.

Tax relief

Interest paid in any tax year on a loan for the purpose of buying, improving, or extending one's home, from whatever source the loan is obtained, is allowable as a deduction from total income before assessment to income tax. The effect of this is to give relief at the top rate of tax paid ('marginal' rate) on the amount of interest paid on house mortgages.

There are certain limitations to this relief. First, it is restricted (up to 1980/81) to interest on a total borrowing of £25,000, no relief being available on interest paid on borrowing over this limit. Second, it is available only on the borrowing on your main residence, not on a second home. If you have a mortgage of £10,000 on your main residence and £8,000 on your holiday home, for instance, you can claim tax relief only on the £10,000 mortgage interest. However, when you are moving house and you take out a mortgage on the new home before paying off the mortgage on the old one, the Inland Revenue will allow tax relief on both mortgages for up to 12 months, providing the old home is vacant and on the market. In such a case your relief is still restricted to interest on a total borrowing of £25,000.

Repayment mortgages

The majority of home buyers elect to repay their mortgage loans by the annuity method, commonly called the 'repayment method'. This provides for the borrower to make regular monthly repayment instalments such that, over the life of the mortgage, the debt, together with interest, is repaid entirely.

Instalments

The amount of the monthly instalment that will apply when the loan is first arranged will, of course, depend partly on the interest rate prevailing at that time.

Example
Monthly repayments on a £10,000 mortgage:

Interest rate	20-year term	25-year term	30-year term
12%	£111.60	£106.30	£103.50
15%	£133.20	£129.00	£127.00

Two points to notice in the above example are that the size of the monthly repayments increases less than proportionately to the rise in interest rates; this is because the amount of capital repayment in total must be a constant. In the above example an interest rate of 15%, which is precisely 25% higher than 12%, results in the repayments being only 19.4% higher (20-year term) or 21.4% higher (25-year term) or 22.8% higher (30-year term). Secondly, monthly instalments on a 25-year term are significantly lower than on a 20-year term, but those on a 30-year term are not much lower than on a 25-year term.

The monthly instalment consists partly of interest and partly of capital repayment. Since the amount of the debt is being reduced continuously, whereas the amount of the monthly instalment remains unchanged, it follows that the early instalments consist very largely of interest, with very little capital repayment; whereas the later instalments will consist mostly of capital repayment, the interest element having fallen since the debt will have been reduced.

As a very rough guide to the cost of servicing a repayment mortgage you may notice that, at an interest rate of 12.5%, the monthly gross repayment before tax relief on a 25-year mortgage is about £10 per £1,000 mortgage.

Effect of tax relief

The fact that a repayment mortgage is a reducing debt is particularly relevant when considering the effect of tax relief on the cost of your mortgage payments. Relief is allowable only on the interest element, not on the capital repayment. In the second example above, with a mortgage of £10,000 over a 25-year period for instance, the initial amount of monthly interest at 15% is (£10,000 × 15) ÷ (100 × 12), or £125, out of the total instalment of £129. With tax relief at basic rate of 30% the real cost of each month's instalment in the first year is thus £129 − £37.50, which is £91.50. But in the 25th year, when the borrowing will have been reduced to only a few hundred pounds, nearly all the monthly repayments will consist of capital, so the tax relief will be almost nil.

The value of tax relief with a repayment mortgage is greatest in the early years, falling progressively throughout the term.

Changes in interest rates

Since mortgage rates go up and down from time to time, albeit less frequently than banks' base rates, one would expect that every borrower would be repeatedly having to change the amount of his monthly repayment. Whilst it is true that this can occur, especially with violent changes in interest rates, in many cases frequent alterations in the amounts of the repayments can be avoided.

When rates rise by a comparatively small step many borrowers are given the option of either appropriately increasing their repayments or of extending the term of the loan. It will readily be comprehended that if the instalment remains unchanged but the interest element included in it becomes higher, then the capital repayment element becomes lower. Thus the mortgage is being repaid more slowly.

In recent years some rises in rates have been so violent that were the repayment instalment not to be increased it would not even cover the interest on the loan, with the consequence that the outstanding loan would be increasing instead of decreasing. However, most borrowers increase their monthly payments rather than extend the life of their loans.

Personal finance

When interest rates fall it is open to borrowers to reduce the monthly payment – especially where the fall is one from a historically very high level such as 15%. However, many borrowers, having accustomed themselves to budgeting for their mortgage repayments, may leave them unchanged, which will result in the mortgage being entirely repaid earlier than originally planned.

True interest rate

Interest on annuity loans is normally charged on what is known as an 'annual rest' basis, *i.e.* the interest in the first year is charged on the initial loan for the period up to the end of the society's financial year. In subsequent years interest is charged for the whole year on the debt outstanding at the beginning of the society's financial year.

The consequence of this is that a borrower is paying interest at the agreed rate on money he is not borrowing, for the amount of the outstanding debt at the beginning of any year is more than the average amount borrowed over the whole year. Unlike short-term personal bank loans, however, where the true interest rate works out at something like twice the flat rate, the result of yearly rests on a long-term loan is quite small. A 15% nominal rate represents a true rate of 16.2%.

Endowment-linked mortgages

There is an alternative to the traditional annuity mortgage, which is the endowment-linked mortgage. The main difference lies in the method of making repayment of the loan.

Under the annuity method the borrower makes gradual repayment of the borrowed capital every month during the term of the mortgage. Under the endowment method *no* capital repayment at all is made to the society, monthly payments being restricted to the interest. Since the amount of the loan does not decrease each month, the amount of interest paid remains unchanged, so long as the interest rate remains unchanged. Repayment of the loan is made in one sum at the end of the term, from the proceeds of an endowment policy on the life of the borrower for the same amount and term as the mortgage. So the borrower must pay a monthly premium on the endowment policy to the insurance company, in addition to the interest to the society.

The policy itself is charged to the building society as security for the borrowing and the society is willing to accept this because (a) if the borrower lives to the end of the term the entire mortgage will be repaid in one sum from the proceeds of the maturing policy, and (b) if the borrower should die in the meantime the mortgage will be repaid entirely from the policy claim proceeds.

The supporting endowment policy may be a full with-profits one, a non-profit one, or a low-cost with-profits policy (*see* Chapter 12). Specimen costings of three different ways of arranging a mortgage are shown in the table on page 98.

A repayment mortgage has one particular advantage over the alternative methods for a person whose budget for the first few years is very tight: the tax relief available during the early years *on the interest element* is as high as it is throughout the term by the endowment method, so his net monthly outgoing for the first year, for example, will be some £9 less than the average amount as shown in the above example, although it will become higher as the years pass.

A disadvantage of the endowment method is that, when interest rates rise, it is not possible for the term to be extended; the higher interest charge must be met in full.

Option mortgages

An 'option' mortgage is one where, instead of the interest payments being allowable for tax relief, the rate of interest actually paid to the society is lower than the normal rate by approximately the basic rate of tax. The difference is paid to the society by the government.

This arrangement is intended to ensure that as much benefit is given to a house buyer who cannot, by reason of the smallness of his taxable income, take full advantage of the tax relief available, as is given to a person with a higher taxable income.

Example

A housebuyer needs a £7,500 mortgage which is offered to him at 12.5%, or at 8.8% on an option mortgage. The buyer's total income is £3,000 a year. A married man, he has a dependent relative, so his personal allowances are £2,145 + £100 = £2,245. He contributes 6% (£216) of income to a company pension plan. Net taxable income is thus £539. Before making the house purchase he will be liable to tax at 30% of £539, which is £161.70

If he accepted a normal repayment mortgage his *interest* payments in the first year would be 12.5% of £7,500, which is £937.50. He would

Example

Alternative methods of repaying a £10,000 mortgage over 25 years

Annuity method		*Low-cost endowment with-profits method*		*Endowment with-profits method*	
[Interest rate 15%]	£	[Interest rate 15.25%]	£	[Interest rate 15.25%]	£
Gross monthly repayment	128.92	Gross monthly interest	127.08	Gross monthly interest	127.08
Average monthly interest £95.59					
less Tax relief	28.68	*less* Tax relief	38.12	*less* Tax relief	38.12
Net average monthly repayment	100.24	Net monthly interest	88.96	Net monthly interest	88.96
		Gross monthly premium £16.65 Paid net of tax relief	13.74	Gross monthly premium £37.75 Paid net of tax relief	31.14
Total net monthly outlay	100.24	Total net monthly outlay	102.70	Total net monthly outlay	120.10
Net outlay over mortgage term	30,072.00	Net outlay over mortgage term	30,810.00	Net outlay over mortgage term	36,030.00
		Deduct balance of estimated bonuses payable to you in cash after mortgage has been repaid	6,260.00	Deduct estimated bonuses payable to you in cash in addition to the guaranteed sum assured which pays off your mortgage	29,200.00
Estimated net total outlay	30,072.00	Estimated net total outlay	24,550.00	Estimated net total outlay	6,830.00

be entitled to tax relief on this sum. But since this exceeds his taxable income the benefit he derives from it is limited to the amount of tax he hitherto paid, namely £161.70. Thus, the net cost of paying the interest is £937.50 less £161.70, which is £775.80.

An option mortgage, on the other hand, will cost him in the first year in interest only 8.8% of £7,500, which is £651.20, a saving of £124.60 in the year.

It pays to take an option mortgage where a borrower's income is such that, after deducting the allowances and the first year's total mortgage interest at normal interest rates, the remaining taxable income is nil.

An option mortgage having been taken it is not, under present legislation, permitted to change to a normal mortgage for a period of one year, so you should consider the likely changes in your taxable income in that year before committing yourself to an option mortgage. Should your income rise to a point where tax at higher rates is payable, an option mortgage will be most disadvantageous.

Top-up mortgages

When the general supply of mortgage funds is insufficient to meet in full all demands for mortgages from qualified would-be borrowers, societies are obliged to ration their funds. Thus, in recent years it has become common to find that a society is restricting all new mortgages to a top figure of £13,000, £17,000 or £19,000, even though the value of the property and the income status of the applicant would justify lending beyond those figures.

Notes to table opposite

1. With an endowment mortgage the building society does not gain the advantage in the interest rate of the margin between agreed rate and true rate (*see* page 96) that arises under the annual rest method of a repayment (annuity) mortgage. However, the society charges a rate of 0.25% higher for an endowment mortgage.

2. In total, considerably more tax relief is available under an endowment-linked mortgage than under a repayment mortgage.

3. In real terms, a full with-profits endowment mortgage is in the long term, a more profitable way of buying a house than the other two methods. However, the monthly outgoing, net of tax relief, is considerably higher.

4. Tax relief is calculated at basic rate (30% for 1980/81).

In such a case it is usually possible to arrange for a life assurance company to lend an additional amount subject to certain restrictions, up to a level of total borrowing that the society itself would have permitted had funds been available. This top-up loan will be secured by a second mortgage on the property in favour of the insurance company.

Interest on top-ups

Rates of interest on the top-up part of the borrowing are usually a point or two above the rate on the basic mortgage, but this is not invariably so. Sometimes the top-up rate is fixed for the duration of the borrowing, or fixed for five years, or it may be variable.

Must be endowment-linked

In every case where a top-up loan is obtained the whole of the borrowing, basic plus top-up, must be covered by endowment policies issued by the topping-up life office. It necessarily follows that the monthly outgoing for any borrowing that includes a top-up is appreciably higher than it would be were the whole amount being borrowed from a building society under a repayment mortgage. A top-up arrangement nevertheless can be a sound and profitable investment provided a good life office is used.

Most life offices will allow the policy covering the basic loan to be with-profits, non-profit, or low-cost. But on the top-up loan it is usual to require the policy to be either full with-profits or non-profit, budget low-cost plans not usually being permitted.

Further advances

Building societies lend, in general, only for the purpose of enabling their members (investors or borrowers) to buy their own homes or to move to another home. Building society mortgages are not available for facilitating the acquisition of a holiday home or for the financing of the purchase of any asset other than a private residence.

It is, nevertheless, normal for an existing borrowing member to be allowed to increase his loan for any purpose that improves the value of the property. For example, further advances (additional lending) may be made for the purpose of installing central heating, building an extension or converting a loft to a room.

In times of mortgage shortage it may be difficult to obtain a further advance, and most societies in any case expect an applicant to put up some money himself. Further advances up to 80% of the cost of improvements are quite common.

Repairs and maintenance

A house owner is expected to keep his house in a good state of repair and condition out of his income. A further advance for making good damage, or wear and tear, or for decorating, is not generally available.

However, where an old property has been purchased on a building society mortgage, and in course of time it is decided that it needs re-roofing, a further advance may still be possible if it can be shown that the work will enhance the value of the property, making it a better house than when it was first bought.

The home loan scheme

There exists a government-sponsored scheme for assisting first-time home buyers. The scheme offers a tax-free bonus and an interest-free loan to those people who have been saving for at least two years under the scheme. In addition to the bonus, of course, normal interest will be paid on the investment by the savings institution.

To take advantage of this scheme a person must agree to save regularly (no minimum amounts are laid down) with any of the many acceptable institutions, including banks, friendly societies, building societies, National Girobank, National Savings Bank and Trustee Savings Banks, and must inform the institution that he wishes to participate in the scheme.

One year before he applies for the bonus he must have at least £300 in his account, and during the succeeding year the balance must never fall below that figure. At the end of the second year he will, if he then takes out a mortgage on a first purchase of a property priced at not above a figure laid down from time to time by the government, qualify to receive:

(*a*)   a tax-free cash bonus, additional to the interest earned, of up to £110, and

(*b*)   provided he has a minimum of £600 in his account, the government will lend him £600 on top of the building society loan, free of interest for five years.

This can be an extremely valuable facility for young, first-time buyers of low-priced properties, since it may enable them to buy a home without first having to save up the full 10% of the purchase price. (The above figures applied in 1980.)

Initial costs of house buying

Buying a house or flat is quite an expensive business. Quite apart from having to find the deposit money in cash, say 10% of the price, and of having to make the regular recurring mortgage payments of interest and repayment (or endowment premium) there are quite substantial initial costs to budget for.

Structural survey

In the case of a new flat or house, or one that is less then 10 years old and on which the builder's 10-year guarantee is still in force, a purchaser may be prepared to accept that the property is free from major faults. For older properties, however, it would be a reasonable precaution to commission an independent, qualified surveyor to make a structural survey to ensure that there are no hidden, serious defects. The fee for this is likely to be between £100 and £200, but there is no set scale.

Building society valuation

A house buyer applying for a building society mortgage loan will have to pay the valuation fee of the surveyor employed by the society. This is additional to the cost of any survey commissioned by the buyer. It should be realised that the inspection by the society's surveyor is *not* a structural survey, but only a valuation for the purpose of confirming that the property is suitable security for the loan. The present scale for valuations is as follows:

Valuation	Fee
Not exceeding £15,000	£5 plus £1 per £500 or part thereof in excess of £2,000
£15,000 to £30,000	£31 plus £1 per £1,000 in excess of £15,000
£30,000 to £40,000	£46 plus £1 per £2,000 in excess of £30,000
Over £40,000	by arrangement

Legal charges

Most of the legal charges will be paid by the purchaser to his solicitor in the first instance, although some will be disbursed to other people. Legal charges will include the following:

Solicitor's services. The charge made by your solicitor for his own services in examining title to the property, advising you, and preparing the conveyance. There is no set fee but a fair average would be 1% of the value of the property.

Land registry fee. If the land on which the property stands is what is called 'registered land', a land registry fee will be payable. If it is not registered land it is likely that the solicitor's own charge will be higher by about the amount of the fee, as his work in checking the deeds is more onerous. Land registry fees are:

Value	Fee
Not exceeding £20,000	£2.50 for every £1,000 or part.
£20,000 to £100,000	£50 for the first £20,000 and £2.40 for every £1,000 or part in excess.
Over £100,000	£242 for the first £100,000 and 50p per £1,000 or part in excess, with a maximum of £567

Stamp duty. A government tax is payable by the purchaser of a property exceeding £20,000. For a property priced at just over £20,000 the tax is payable on the whole amount, not just on the excess. Rates are as follows:

Not over £20,000	Free
£20,000 to £25,000	25p per £50 or part thereof
£25,000 to £30,000	50p per £50 or part thereof
£30,000 to £35,000	75p per £50 or part thereof
Over £35,000	£1 per £50 or part thereof

Duty is calculated on the whole value at the rate indicated, not at different rates on successive slices.

Mortgage deed. The charge for the preparation of the mortgage deed, which will be made by the building society's solicitor, will, where the same solicitor acts for both society and purchaser, be on the following scale, based on the amount of the mortgage, not the value of the property. The buyer must reimburse the society for this.

Personal finance

Specimen charges for mortgage deed

Advance (£)	Charge (£)
3,000	20
4,000	24
5,000	29
8,000	40
10,000	45
15,000	50
20,000	54
25,000	57

Value added tax. VAT at 15% (1980/81) is payable on solicitor's own charges and on solicitor's mortgage charge, and also on the valuation fee.

Mortgage guarantee premium. Where the loan exceeds (usually) 80% of the valuation a premium will be payable, once only, on the excess lending at rates quoted on page 92.

Example

Mr George Jamieson has to move house and agrees to purchase a three-year old property on registered land for £35,000 on which the builder's 10-year guarantee is still current. A mortgage of £15,000 is arranged with a building society. In addition to his own removal expenses, and the commission he will pay to the estate agent for the selling of his old home, what will be the approximate initial costs of making the move?

Answer	£
Survey not necessary	
Building society valuation	49
Own solicitor probably about	350
Land registry fee	86
Stamp duty at 2%	700
Mortgage deed	50
VAT on £350 + £50 + £49	
= £449 at 15%	67.35
	1,302.35

TEST QUESTIONS

1. What proportion of the purchase price of a £25,000 property might a borrower hope to borrow from a building society?
2. In what way does the size of your income set a limit to the amount you can borrow from a building society?
3. Is the building society mortgage interest fixed or variable?
4. What limitations are there on the tax relief available on the interest paid on home loans?

5. Distinguish between a repayment mortgage and an endowment-linked mortgage

6. In the case of a repayment mortgage, tax relief is high in the early years, falling continuously year by year. Why is this?

7. In times of high interest rates some building society borrowers find that their debt is increasing instead of decreasing. Why is this? What can be done to rectify the situation?

8. What is an option mortgage?

9. What is a top-up mortgage and under what circumstances can such a facility be of use?

10. For what purpose other than buying a house may a building society be willing to lend money?

11. Describe the government-sponsored 'home loan' scheme.

12. Describe, without quantifying, the main 'one-off' initial costs that must be met when buying a house with the aid of a building society mortgage.

EXERCISES

A Harry and Julia Newton earn basic pay of £4,800 and £3,500 a year respectively. Under Harry's terms of employment he is entitled to a bonus that varies in amount but which has averaged £600 a year over the last three years; £400 of this is guaranteed. A building society has indicated that on an earnings basis it would consider an application for a £16,750 mortgage on the joint incomes under normal conditions, but that with interest levels of 15% the total borrowing would be restricted to £13,675. Show the society's calculations of these amounts. Could the couple hope to get a top-up loan to bring the total borrowing to a higher level? Give reasons for the answer.

B What will be the single premium on the mortgage guarantee that will be required for a mortgage loan of £24,000 on a property valued at £27,000, where the rules of the society require independent security to be taken for the excess lending over 80% of valuation? Assume the premium rate to be 4%.

C What will be the net cost after tax relief to a basic-rate taxpayer of the first complete year's instalments on a 25-year repayment mortgage for £10,000, basing your answer on the specimen figures on page 98)?

D What will be the approximate initial costs involved in purchasing a property valued at the purchase price of £18,000, and obtaining a 90% mortgage on it from a building society? Base your answer on pages 102 to 104, and include the mortgage guarantee premium.

PART FOUR

Personal expenditure

9 Types of expenditure

Every business has to budget its expenditure. It has to estimate as accurately as it can what cash it will need to spend, on which items in what quantities and in what time periods. It also has to ensure, as far as possible, that its inward flow of cash from its customers, together with its cash stock, is going to be sufficient to meet all calls made upon it as they arise.

A private individual is in much the same position. He also has to budget his expenditure in such a way that his flow of income, plus his stock of cash, is going to be adequate to see him through.

Fixed and variable expenditure

To help in framing your budget it is useful to make a distinction between those items of current expenditure that are fixed, at least in the short to medium term, and those that are variable, that can within reason be lowered or raised according to how you plan your activities. Fixed expenditure is said to be 'time-based' in that it is proportional to time; variable expenditure is said to be 'activity-based' in that it can be expanded or contracted according to your decisions on what to do and what not to do.

In the case of a business, for instance, the fixed expenditure or costs will include rent and rates on premises, interest payable on borrowed capital, insurance of premises, machinery and stock, and the minimum costs of telephone, heating, lighting and power needed to keep the business in existence. None of these costs can be reduced without causing the business to collapse, or to contract significantly.

The remaining expenditure will vary more or less in direct proportion with the level of activity of the firm. In a time of expansion purchases of stock and materials will rise, stock carried will need to be higher, wages will increase as will cost of power consumed, telephone, administrative staff, postage, labelling, transport and so on.

Personal costs

To analyse expenditure into fixed and variable can be a useful device also when considering personal and individual budgets. A householder's fixed expenditure will often include the following:

mortgage instalments (or rent);
household rates and water rates;
heating (partly variable as it is possible to economise but not to reduce to nil);
lighting;
telephone;
maintenance, licensing and insuring the car;
fares to work;
insurance of property and contents;
life assurance premium.

None of these items can be reduced significantly except by making drastic and long-term changes in lifestyle, such as moving to a cheaper house, changing job, having the telephone disconnected or getting rid of the car. It is, of course, true that many forms of expenditure share the qualities of being fixed and variable: they can be voluntarily rationed and so could be termed 'semi-variable' – one can lower the thermostat of the central heating, switch off more lights, cut down on telephone conversations.

Other expenditure is capable of being tailored to what we can afford to pay. The amount we spend on the following items is variable because even in the short term we can reduce it:

food and drink;
eating out;
clothing replacements;
car running costs;
holidays and entertainment;
maintenance of property;
giving presents.

Budgeting

To draft out a budget of income and expenditure is a simple way of ensuring that you will not commit yourself to spending more than you earn.

Specimen monthly budget of a young married couple living on a single income

Revenue	£	Expenditure	£
Net take-home pay		Mortgage instalment	110
after tax, NI contri-		Rates and water rate	20
butions and		Gas	8
company pension		Electricity	7
contributions	420	Telephone	10
		Property insurance	4
		Contents insurance	2
		Car overheads:	
		Licence £60 p.a.	
		Insurance £75 p.a.	
		Maintenance £105 p.a.	
		£240 divide by 12	20
		TV licence at £34 p.a.	3
		Fares to work	40
		Life assurance (net)	11
		Total fixed expenditure	235
		Thus available for variable	
		expenditure	185
	420		420

If in this example the couple's expenditure on food comes to around £100 a month, and if clothing replacements average £20 a month, petrol, oil, tyres and batteries costing another £20, there will be £45 a month left over for holidays, entertainment, eating out, property repairs, decorating and spending money, as well as an amount for saving. The budget may seem a bit tight; possibly an economy holiday will have to be taken in the present year. It's up to each household how best to lay out the available money to get the most satisfaction.

Revenue and capital expenditure

Most of our items of daily expenditure consist, in number if not not in value, of purchases of consumer goods and services. By consumer goods we mean goods that are completely used up in one go, such as food and drink, bus fares, chocolate, petrol and hairdos, visits to the cinema or football matches. We pay for these out of our current income or revenue, for which reason such items of expenditure may be termed 'revenue expenditure'. On the other hand, some of the things we buy, although usually classified as consumer goods, are not used up immediately, but gradually over a comparatively short period of years. These include clothing, shoes, some toys and sports equipment – things that wear out comparatively quickly.

Capital goods

At the other extreme we also spend money on capital goods. The classic example of capital goods is land. Land never wears out and never needs replacing, yet it yields a benefit to its owner in perpetuity. The biggest item of capital expenditure that most of us ever make is the purchase of a house and garden. The house itself, although it will not last for ever, is likely to preserve its value at least for a lifetime, yielding a continuous supply of utility to the owner in the form of shelter, warmth and comfort.

Domestic capital expenditure

Other examples of capital expenditure are purchases of carpets, furniture and fittings for the home, TV and radio sets, cars, washing machines, dishwashers, refrigerators, music centres and cameras. The purchase of any of these is an investment in a productive capital asset – productive in the sense that its use will produce not an income over a period of time, but a stream of utilities. Such assets are often called 'consumer durables' because they share the qualities of both consumer goods and capital goods.

Like most capital assets such goods depreciate over time, and their useful life is limited to a fairly short period of years, at the end of which they become valueless or of scrap value only, and have to be replaced. Over the long term, therefore, a wise individual will make provision for replacing them as they wear out, setting aside regular savings from income to meet the eventual cost.

Inflation

In times of rapidly rising prices the calculation of how much cash to set aside for replacing capital assets is very difficult. If an asset has a projected life of, say, eight years, one's first thought would be that it should be sufficient to set aside each year one-eighth of its cost. This may prove to be insufficient for two main reasons: (a) that as the years pass the cost of repair and maintenance is likely to increase as the object is getting older; and (b) in eight years' time the price of a replacement may have about doubled. However, if in eight years it *has* doubled, it is likely that one's money income will also have doubled. In other words it would be reasonable to set aside each year rather more than one-eighth *not* of the original cost price, but of the rising replacement cost year by year. For a short-life asset a fraction with a denominator of 1 lower than the projected life will probably suffice. In this case that would make it one-seventh.

Example

An asset costs £400 today and has a projected life of five years. Inflation is expected to average 10% over the five years and it is assumed that both replacement cost and money income will rise by the same amount. The following action would spread the burden of provision evenly over the years:

	Cost	Year's provision (¼)
	£	£
1st year	400	100
2nd year	440	110
3rd year	484	121
4th year	532	133
5th year	585	146
		610

Some slight over-provision will have been made, but this might just about balance the rising costs of repairs in the fifth year.

Nobody can forecast for longer than a few months what the rate of inflation is likely to be. So the above figures are intended only to illustrate that maintenance and replacement costs of wasting assets are likely to be a great deal higher than an unsophisticated appraisal might suggest, and to indicate one way in which they might be provided for.

Capital formation

It might be thought that since revenue expenditure is financed out of revenue (income), then capital expenditure is necessarily financed out of a stock of money capital derived from past savings. This is not necessarily the case. Although it is true that if expenditure on consumer goods exceeds income we are necessarily spending capital (either by running down our own money balances or by increasing our debt to other people), the parallel does not hold true for capital expenditure. This can, and very often is, financed out of current revenue. A couple of illustrations will make this clear.

House purchase

Clearly buying a house is capital expenditure. But if a deposit is paid of only £2,000, being 10% of the purchase price of £20,000, the remainder being raised on a mortgage loan, then £18,000 worth of house is being paid for out of present and future income. In other words you are contracting to save out of income over a period of years to pay for the capital expenditure being incurred today. Of course this privilege costs more, in the form of interest on the loan. But if interest averages 10% a year (7% after tax relief at basic rate), and house values rise by 10% a year, the real cost of buying now rather than later is nil – indeed is less than nil.

If, instead of buying a house, you rent it, then you certainly acquire the sole right of enjoyment of the capital asset, but no investment is being made; no capital formation is taking place; rent is a revenue expenditure on a consumer good. The rent, being paid out of income, is simply a purchase of a current service, like the cost of going to the pictures.

Purchase of TV set

Buying a car is capital expenditure whether you buy it entirely for cash or by a down payment with the balance in monthly instalments on hire purchase. Again, the fact that the monthly instalments are financed out of current income does not make the acquisition of the asset an item of current expenditure.

The same principle applies with a TV set: you can buy it for cash, or by hire purchase or credit agreement. But there is a third method of acquiring the use of a TV set – or indeed of many similar items of capital equipment – you can hire it for a simple rent. The equipment will never become your property, of course, since you are merely renting it. There are some advantages in choosing this method: you don't have to pay for servicing, repairs, replacement of tube or maintenance, and you can usually change the set, at an additional cost, for an up-to-date one when it becomes out-dated. Cost-wise there is little to choose between the cost of rental on the one hand and the total costs of purchasing, which are:

(a) either interest forfeited on the money laid out on a cash purchase, or the monthly interest element in a hire purchase agreement.

(b) insurance against accident, damage and parts replacement;

(c) servicing;

(d) depreciation.

As with a house, if you rent a TV set your payments are revenue expenditure – you are buying a current service. If you buy a TV set your payments are capital expenditure – you are buying an asset that will give you a yield in terms of services.

Business accounts

The distinction between revenue expenditure and capital expenditure is very important in the accounts of a business, as will be seen in Chapter 13 on interpretation of accounts. Capital expenditure results in, or is due to, the acquisition of permanent assets, which must appear in the balance sheet, while revenue expenditure represents the expenses of running the business – purchases of materials, wages, selling expenses, etc. – and is charged to the trading or profit and loss account.

TEST QUESTIONS
1. Explain the distinction between personal fixed expenditure and personal variable expenditure.
2. Is the rent payable on furnished accommodation fixed or variable?
3. Distinguish between revenue and capital expenditure. How would you classify the hire purchase instalments on the purchase of a new car?
4. Give one example of expenditure that is financed out of current income but is nevertheless capital expenditure.
5. What is a consumer durable?
6. Consider the advantages and disadvantages in times of inflation of purchasing assets on an instalment plan instead of (a) renting or hiring, and (b) saving up out of income to buy for cash later on.

EXERCISES
A You buy a second-hand car for £520 cash. You estimate that its

useful life will be five years, and that at the end of that time it will be worthless. You also anticipate that prices and your own income will rise by 12.5% for each of the next five years. Prepare a table showing how much cash to set aside out of income each year to pay for a replacement. Ignore the rising cost of servicing and repairs.

B You estimate that out of your take-home net pay you are spending the following amounts each month:

	£
Accommodation and food (living at home)	42
Budget account at clothing outfitter	12
HP on motorbike	22
Petrol and oil	15
Midday meals	15
Spending money	20

Which items are capital expenditure and which revenue expenditure?
Which items would you classify as variable and which fixed?
How much per month are you saving, and how do you plan to replace the motorbike when it wears out in seven years' time.?

10 Accommodation

The cost of accommodation is a major item in everybody's budget. For a couple buying their own house or flat the monthly expenditure on mortgage instalments is by no means the only cost involved in occupying the property. Whilst the mortgage payments may be considered to be capital expenditure in the sense that they are payment for a capital asset that has been purchased even though the money is being found from current income, all other expenses of accommodation are pure revenue expenditure.

Fixed expenditure

Items of fixed expenditure inseparable from the occupying of your own property include the following.

(a)   If the property is leasehold there will be a ground rent payable to the landlord, usually the owner of the free-hold. The amount of this may be merely nominal as in the case of many newly built flats having a 99-year or 999-year lease, or it may be a substantial figure. For example, a one-bedroom flat in London's West End might be advertised at a price of £20,000, but it could well turn out that the purchaser will only get a 10-year leasehold, on the termination of which possession reverts to the freeholder. And during those 10 years a ground rent of possible £2,000 a year may be payable in addition to the initial capital outlay of £20,000.

(b)   Rates and water rates are payable to the local authority and water authority respectively (*see* Chapter 3) by the registered occupier of the property, whether owner or tenant. Although rates are assessed as a percentage of rateable value, in terms of cash payable they are likely to be more than 0.5% a year of the market value of the property. Rates on a £20,000 flat with a long lease might well cost £120 a year or £10 a month.

(c)　You will need to insure the property against fire and damage. Commonly the premium will be at an annual rate of up to 0.2% of the insured value, which ought to be not less than the market value. For a flat valued at £22,000, therefore, property insurance is likely to cost up to £44 a year, or nearly £4 a month.

(d)　In the case of many purpose-built flats an annual 'service charge' is payable by the leaseholder to the freeholder or to a residents' association. This is designed to meet the costs of repairs, exterior decoration, and maintenance of the stairways, lifts and other common parts of the building.

(e)　Comprehensive insurance of household contents will cost about 0.25% a year of the insured value. The likely cost of replacing new all the contents of a three-bedroomed house would lie between £3,000 and £10,000, so this is not an item to be neglected in any budget.

Variable expenditure

As well as the fixed expenditure connected with property, there are many other calls on your budget associated with accommodation.

Maintenance

Whilst a short-term wasting asset, such as a car, depreciates in value by as much as 33% per annum (new car) or an average of 20% per annum (over four years old), freehold property does not depreciate in value if it is well built and well looked after. Nevertheless, it does require continual, if irregular, expenditure on it in repairs and maintenance.

It will need complete redecoration inside and out every few years, or its value will fall. If contractors are employed for this purpose the outside decoration could cost a thousand pounds, the inside a hundred or so per room. DIY would be a great deal cheaper but materials alone are likely to cost £15 a room for paint, or several multiples of that for papering. The outside can

117

be given a coat of paint quite economically but the project makes great demands on one's time, skill and patience with ladders. If outside paintwork is allowed to deteriorate beyond a certain point all the old paint will need removing. This is a big and expensive job.

Repairs

Redecorating the outside is likely to reveal defects in wood-work, gutters and pipes, parts of which may be found to have rotted or rusted. All such damage has to be made good to ensure that the property does not lose value. Newly built houses are, as one would expect, likely to need the least expenditure on repairs and renewals, but as the years pass the expense mounts up. Properties over 30 to 40 years old some-times need the roofing slates or tiles to be replaced; Edwardian houses often need completely re-roofing, inclu-ding replacing the roof timbers. This can run into thousands of pounds.

Improvements

The cost of extensions, conversions or improvements to your home, as distinguished from maintenance work, are treated rather differently, for they represent capital expenditure since they increase the value of the asset. Costs of extensions are high; during 1980 a fair average price for permanent brick-built extensions worked out at between £22 and £35 per square foot of floor area, depending on area and on whether the work involved alterations or installations of electric wiring and plumbing. To this must be added incidental costs such as those of obtaining planning permission, possibly of architect's fees and certainly the cost of having detailed drawings and specifications prepared in order to submit the application for local authority approval. Drawings will be needed for approval under the local authority's building regulations even though the extension may be a minor one not subject to full planning approval. Another possible expense might well be the charge that some local authorities will be making, from April 1981, for the consideration of planning proposals. When the improve-ment has been completed it is likely that the rateable value will be increased.

Wooden extensions or the erection of sun-rooms are much cheaper than traditional brick-built extensions, but it is an open question whether such additions to a house increase the value of the asset to any appreciable extent. A building society is unlikely to be willing to grant a further advance on a wooden extension, but finance over two or three years can usually be obtained, at a price, from a hire-purchase or finance company.

Rented accommodation

Unfurnished houses and flats to rent are not often available in the private sector, partly because recent legislation discourages an owner from letting to a tenant. Furnished accommodation, however, is generally available where it consists of a part only of a single dwelling partly occupied by the landlord.

Unfurnished

An unfurnished house or flat is unlikely to be offered to let by the owner for a rent that does not give him a reasonable return on his capital. As an alternative to letting the property the owner could sell it and invest the proceeds to yield interest. If the market value of the property is £30,000 he could place the proceeds in gilt-edged stock to earn the going rate of long-term interest. In 1980 this was around 11% or 12%, so a landlord would expect a rent that will give him at least an equivalent yield.

It is usual for a landlord to be responsible for repairs and renewals and renovations in the case of unfurnished accommodation on a long let, and also for the external decoration – always subject to the terms of the particular agreement. So he will need to allow for this in the rent charged. If he estimates that repairs and maintenance are going to cost him another 1% of the market value then he might ask a rent of around 13% or so of the value, which would be £3,900 a year, or £325 a month – not very different from the monthly outgoing on a £30,000 mortgage over 25 years.

That being the case, a seeker of property would be likely to choose to buy rather than rent, for by doing so he will, at the end of 25 years, have paid out the same amount of money as he would have paid in rent, but will then be the owner of a mortgage-free asset. Rent payments are revenue expenditure; mortgage repayments are capital expenditure.

However, this thought will not have escaped the attention of the landlord. The return he will obtain from letting the property instead of selling it will consist not *only* of net rent, but also of capital appreciation in money terms, for the value of the property is likely to rise at least in line with inflation. The owner of a property holds an appreciating asset. So a landlord is likely to abate the rent he demands for a property by an amount representing at least a proportion of the capital gain, otherwise he would get no takers. The rent in practice is likely to be around the £2,400 mark, or £200 a month.

For unfurnished lets the landlord is responsible for the insurance of the property, in most cases, but it is the tenant who must pay the rates, electricity, gas, oil and telephone.

Council property

The terms for tenancy of council property are on a different footing in most cases. In the first place, the standard rent is generally based not on market value of the property but on the original cost, often a very great deal lower, on the grounds that the person who should benefit from the escalation in property prices since the date of construction should be the tenant and not the landlord (the council). From a purely commercial point of view the tenant is obtaining a service from the council at a price subsidised by the general ratepayers of the area, for it is their council that had the good sense to invest in house property, and it could be argued that the benefit should be spread among all ratepayers, not just those occupying council property.

The rent payable on council property commonly includes rates, but this is by no means invariable. One should always read very carefully the draft wording of any agreement for property letting.

Furnished accommodation

It is very difficult to generalise on the terms of agreements for renting furnished accommodation. A very usual such letting is on the basis that the tenant pays for his own metered electricity and gas, and for the telephone, but the landlord pays the rates, water rates, insurance, repairs, maintenance and decoration inside and out. For a fully-furnished house let on this basis the rent will have to be high enough for the landlord to meet all his costs, as well as the wear and tear of his furniture and fittings, out of his rent receipts before he calculates the rate of return on his capital. If the property were lettable unfurnished at £300 a month, the rent for a short-term furnished let is likely to be around £400 a month.

By the same token the rent for a furnished one-bedroom flatlet in any of the big cities is likely to be upwards of £25 a week, or £120 a month. If the rent is expressed as inclusive of all services such as electricity, gas and central heating, as well as of rates, it would be a great deal higher.

TEST QUESTIONS

1. What is meant by the term 'ground rent'?
2. What are the main fixed costs associated with an owner-occupied property?
3. In the case of a house let unfurnished to a short-term tenant, which of the fixed costs are usually payable by the landlord?
4. Name some of the items of variable expenditure associated with the owning of property. Which of these would usually be payable by the landlord in the case of leasehold property?
5. What is a 'service charge' payable by the owner of a leasehold flat?
6. A freehold property that is well looked after does not depreciate significantly in value, even in times of stable prices. Discuss this statement and say whether it would be true in the case of a 900-year leasehold and a 10-year leasehold. If the statement is untrue in such cases, what provision could be made by the lease-holder to ensure he is not homeless at the expiry of the lease?

EXERCISE

Julian Whitehead is offered a flat at a price of £16,000. Enquiry shows that what is being offered is a leasehold with 16 years to run. A ground rent is payable to the landlord of £420 a year, and there is a service charge at present of £25 a quarter. The flat is assessed to rates at £150 and rates plus water rates are 85p in the £. Property insurance will cost Julian 0.15% plus a policy charge of £2. Julian is able to pay cash for the purchase out of money received from a legacy, at present earning interest at 15% gross.

What will be Julian's annual fixed revenue expenditure on the property if he decides to take it? Ignore contents insurance. What additional annual amount should Julian notionally add to this outgoing to determine the real yearly cost to him of owning the flat? Will Julian's capital expenditure on the purchase of the lease provide him with an appreciating asset, or a depreciating asset? Explain your reasons for the answer.

11 Indirect tax

Direct tax, in the form of income tax, local authority rates, capital gains tax and capital transfer tax, were discussed in Chapter 3. These are taxes the burden of which is borne by those people who pay the taxes. But there are other taxes which, because those who initially pay them are able to pass the burden on to other people, are called 'indirect taxes'. These are taxes on goods and services paid by the suppliers but recovered from the eventual consumers of the products in the form of higher prices.

Individuals are less conscious of the incidence of indirect tax than they are of direct tax, because the burden is concealed in the retail price. It may come as a surprise to many to learn that, on average, one-seventh of all the money they spend on goods and service is tax. And it is tax paid out of their incomes that have already been charged to income tax!

National Insurance contributions

National Insurance contributions were treated in some detail in Chapters 1 and 2. Here we merely draw attention to the point that, if these contributions are regarded as a tax (and there are differences of view on this), then the employee's contribution is a direct tax since he cannot pass it on, but the employer's contribution is an indirect tax, since he naturally has to cover the cost of it in the prices he charges for his output. His NI contributions are a part of his overall cost of employing labour.

NI surcharge

The employer of labour also has to pay a tax on all wages he pays, called a 'surcharge', of 3.5%. This is also a part of the cost of hiring labour and has to be recovered in prices. Although this wages tax is paid in the first instance along with his employer's NI contributions, this is purely for the administrative convenience of the authorities. The amount is passed on by the Department of Social Security to the Inland Revenue.

Value added tax

Value added tax (VAT) is an addition to the price of almost all goods and services purchased except food, rent, books and newspapers, and a few other items. In 1980 the rate of this tax was 15%. In most cases the displayed and advertised prices of goods in the shops include the VAT. In some cases of services, however – for example, hotel tariffs, telephone bills, and professional fees of solicitors and surveyors – VAT at 15% is payable in addition to the quoted fees.

In the year 1978/79 VAT produced a revenue for the government of £4,837 million.

It has to be realised that VAT is payable on the full retail price; so goods that have already borne a commodity tax are subject to tax on tax.

Motor car tax

A licence fee of £60 a year has to be paid by the registered owner of any private motor vehicle driven on the public highway. But that is by no means the end of taxation of the motorist.

Before he even puts the vehicle on the road the buyer of a new car will have paid, in the purchase price, a 10% special car tax levied on its manufacture. VAT, of course, is chargeable on the whole retail price, including the 10% car tax. So a car costing the buyer £3,795 will include £495 VAT and £300 car tax. The £60 licence fee per year is payable in addition.

Car tax alone totalled £381 million in 1978/79.

Commodity taxes

Petrol tax

The motorist isn't excused further impost. There is also the duty on hydrocarbon oil products. Each gallon of petrol bought at the pump for £1.35 includes a petroleum tax of 45½p. In 1978/79, when the tax was only 35p, the government obtained a revenue from this source of £2,470 million.

Tobacco

Another money-spinner for the government is tobacco tax, which yielded another £2.5 billion in 1978/79. In 1980 the retail price of a packet of 20 king-size cigarettes included tobacco tax of 52p.

Alcohol

Another major earner is tax on alcoholic drinks. This produces just under £2.5 billion a year. Whoever drinks a pint of beer in 1980/81 contributes 9½p to the Exchequer.

Other indirect taxes

There are other special taxes producing much less revenue. These include imposts on gaming and betting (yield £338 million in 1978/79), customs and excise duties (£736 million in 1978/79), and several lesser items.

In the year 1978/79 indirect tax produced a total income for the government of £14 billion, compared with a yield of £24 billion from direct tax. (An aim of the 1979 Conservative government is to shift some of the burden of direct tax to indirect tax.)

Most commodity taxes are calculated on the *quantity* of the commodity, not on its price. These are called 'specific' taxes. Examples are tobacco, alchohol and petrol. Others are charged on an *ad valorem* basis (*e.g.* customs duties, betting tax), thus as prices rise, so does tax. VAT, of course, is an *ad valorem* tax.

Commodity taxes are taxes on *expenditure* as distinguished from taxes on income. They can, therefore, be avoided by anybody prepared to forgo the taxed products. Non-smokers, non-drinkers, and non-motorists thus avoid a great deal of indirect tax payment. But even they cannot escape VAT unless they are willing to confine their expenditure to food, rent, books and newspapers and a few other essentials.

TEST QUESTIONS
1. Describe the essential characteristic of an indirect tax.
2. Distinguish between specific and *ad valorem* commodity taxes.
3. Do you take the view that wages are subject to indirect taxes? Give your reasons.
4. What is the current rate of VAT? On what goods and services is it levied?

5. Describe the taxes paid by a car owner.
6. Which two commodities yield the largest tax revenue to the government?

EXERCISES

A In a certain week you pay £16 in rent, buy three pints of beer, four gallons of petrol at £1.35 per gallon, £13 worth of food from the supermarket, two books at £2.50 each, and a record for £2.38. Estimate the total of indirect tax that you will have paid.

B Alfred Brown's income is chargeable to income tax at 30%. He buys a new car at a price of £4,427.50 (ignoring delivery charges, number plates, etc.). Including the income tax he will have paid on earning the money with which to buy this car Alfred calculates that the total tax he will have suffered on acquiring his new asset will be £2,427.50. Check this calculation.

12 Insurance

Insurance is a system under which a large number of people pay a regular sum of money into a common pool, the money being used for the purpose of compensating those of them who suffer a loss. In other words, insurance is a scientifically planned method of sharing a financial risk.

Suppose that in a given year 10,000 people buy new bicycles each costing £80. No purchaser, let us say, is willing to risk having his bicycle stolen and having to find the money to buy another one. To meet this problem an organisation has been set up whereby each owner may pay into a fund £1 a year, and in return the fund will pay out £80 to any subscriber whose bicycle gets stolen in that year. If all 10,000 people join the scheme the total annual contributions, called 'premiums', will amount to £10,000. And if, in one year, 100 bicycles are stolen then the total compensation paid to the owners will amount to £8,000; in addition the organisation will have to meet its operating costs. It will probably make a small profit, and the bicycle owners will all have enjoyed peace of mind.

Premiums

Calculating the proper amount for the premium payable for insuring against any risk is very complex. It involves measuring the degree of risk, which itself requires an assessment to be made of the likelihood of a certain event, such as theft, arising in a given period, usually a year. Insurance companies employ expert staff called actuaries and underwriters who, from analyses of past records and current trends, calculate the probabilities of an event occurring, and the average number and sizes of claims likely to arise. Where risk is high the premium will be high. Thus, the premium for insuring a hundred-year-old firework factory against fire will be higher than for a modern brick-built toy factory equipped with automatic sprinklers. The cost of insurance (the premium) bears a direct relationship to the risk.

Insurance can be divided into two main kinds, general (or non-life) insurance, and life insurance. There is a difference in the essential objectives of the two types, and the basic distinction will be more readily comprehended if we first of all describe general insurance.

The indemnity principle

The principle behind general insurance is that the insured person, in return for paying the agreed premium, shall be 'indemnified' should he suffer the loss insured against. To be indemnified means to be placed as nearly as possible in the same position as he would have been in had the loss not occurred. In other words, he is to be 'compensated'. He cannot *gain* by insurance: the maximum claim he can make will be the actual loss he has suffered. So if the peril being insured against is that of having one's £80 bicycle stolen, the compensation he will receive, should that event occur three years later, will be limited to the cost price today of a new bicycle less wear and tear over three years – in other words, to the price of a second-hand bike, say £40.

It therefore follows that, since the value of the article is likely to be worth successively less each year, the premium payable should fall each year. Provided that premium *rates* remain the same, this is exactly what has happened in the past.

New for old

However, in the current inflationary conditions, when the cost of replacing an article is likely to be a great deal higher than the original cost of the damaged or lost article, it is possible to arrange 'a 'new-for-old' contract of insurance. Under this scheme the annual premium will be related to the current new replacement cost, so will naturally rise each year. In return, your insurance claim, should you suffer the loss of the insured item, will amount to the sum needed to buy a new replacement instead of a second-hand bicycle of the same age and condition as the lost one.

Household insurance – buildings

Your home, whether leasehold flat or freehold house, is almost certainly your most valuable possession. Few of us could face the prospect at having to replace it unaided should it be destroyed by fire. Fortunately, the odds against this occurring are very high, so the costs of insuring against the peril are reasonably low (*see* page 117).

Most forms of household insurance cover risks of damage to or destruction of the buildings, permanent fixtures and fittings and decorations, and usually extend to include outbuildings such as garages, sheds and greenhouses. Boundary walls, fences, drives and pathways can be included but may be excluded. Policies vary.

The risks covered are usually those of fire, lightning, explosion, earthquake, theft and malicious damage, storm, tempest, flood, escape of water from pipes and cisterns, and subsidence and landslip. All policies cover impact damage caused by road vehicles, horses and cattle, and damage caused by collapse of aerials and things dropped from aircraft; some will cover damage to the building caused by falling trees. It is usual for the policy to cover breakage of fixed glass (windows, doors, etc.) and fixed sanitary ware and bathroom fittings.

Variation in cover

Policies vary greatly in the extent of perils included, and it is important for the terms of the policy to be studied very carefully. Where the standard contract does not offer cover for some hazard you particularly wish to be insured against, you can usually arrange for the necessary addition to be made, for which you would have to pay an additional premium.

The 'excess' clause

Where the insured person agrees to bear the cost of the first £10, £50 or other stipulated value of any damage or loss, the premium will be appropriately lower. A clause in an insurance to this effect is called an 'excess' clause, derived from the fact that it is only the excess of the damage above the agreed amount that is insured. Many standard contracts contain 'excess' clauses for certain perils, especially contracts for car insurance and for personal effects.

Index linking

As house prices seem set to rise every year it is necessary to ensure that your property insurance stays up to date. A house bought five years ago for £15,000 might now cost £30,000 to rebuild if it were completely destroyed. Many companies now offer an index-linked policy whereby both the insured amount and the renewal premium rise each year at the same rate as the average rise in building costs.

Household insurance – contents

Whether you own your own home or merely rent it unfurnished, you will need to insure the contents – furniture, furnishings, clothing and all the other objects indispensable to the running of a household.

To replace the contents of the average home, should they be destroyed, will cost some thousands of pounds, and their insurance is not included in the buildings insurance policy.

The risks covered by most contents insurance policies follow the same lines as the buildings insurance, with the addition of accidental damage to mirrors, fixed glass in and glass tops of furniture and, in many cases, accidental damage to television sets.

The buildings policy will indemnify the policyholder as owner, and the contents policy will indemnify the policyholder as occupier, against all sums which the insured becomes liable to pay as damages in respect of:

(*a*)   bodily injury (including death or disease); and
(*b*)   loss or destruction of or damage to property belonging to third parties.

Personal liability

An interesting addition to most contents insurances is that of personal liability insurance. If you are responsible for injuring somebody or somebody else's property, you will usually be covered for your legal liability up to £250,000.

Valuation

Remember that you have the option of insuring contents either on the traditional 'indemnity' principle, or on the new-for-old principle.

If you accept the former basis you can claim the cost of repairing damaged articles, or of replacing what has been lost or stolen *less* an amount for wear and tear and depreciation since their purchase. If you accept the latter basis you will be paid the full amount of repairs or the cost of replacing with equivalent new items.

To decide for how much to insure the contents of your home you will have to list every major item in the house and make general 'guesstimates' for the many bits and pieces. Then you value them either at their current value as used items (if using the indemnity basis) or at their current retail replacement prices in the shops (if using the 'new-for-old' basis). The premium will be calculated as a percentage of the value.

All-risks insurance

Contents temporarily removed from the home are afforded limited cover under most policies. However, you should read the terms of the contract very carefully; you will probably discover that valuable items such as jewellery, cameras and sports equipment that are regularly taken out of the house are not covered for accidental loss or damage. If you want to have this 'all risks' cover you will probably be asked for an additional premium.

Motor insurance

It is an offence to drive any motor vehicle on a public highway unless the driver is insured against liability for injuries to other people, including his own passengers, resulting from a traffic accident.

The usual minimum motor insurance, often referred to as 'third-party cover', extends the cover to include not only damage or injury to other persons but also to their property, for example to their vehicles. Thus, should you be involved in an accident that is at least partly your fault, your liability for the damage you cause to the other vehicle will be covered, although the damage to your own vehicle is not covered.

Motor comprehensive

A common addition to the simple third-party insurance is cover against fire and theft of your own vehicle, but not against any other hazards. A full comprehensive policy will give cover against all accidental loss or damage to your car, excluding normal wear and tear and mechanical or electrical breakdown.

Comprehensive cover also usually includes personal accident cover up to a stated limit for yourself and spouse arising from car travel, in any vehicle, including the cost of medical treatment not given by the Health Service. Loss or damage to personal effects carried in the car is also usually included.

Premiums

All motor insurance is expensive, because traffic accidents and car thefts are becoming more and more commonplace and repairs more expensive. Naturally, the greater the hazards insured against, the higher the premium.

As with all general (non-life) insurance the premiums are calculated according to the insurance company's assessment of the degree of risk it is undertaking. Factors taken into consideration in making this assessment include the following.

(*a*)   Make of car, and its type (*e.g.* saloon, sports, racing).

(*b*)   Its overall size, weight and engine capacity.

(*c*)   Where the vehicle is usually kept – in a locked garage or on the street, in a congested town area or in the country.

(*d*)   The age of the driver, the length of time he or she has held a full driving licence, and his or her track record of accident-free motoring.

(*e*)   Whether one named driver or any driver will be in charge of the car.

(*f*)   The occupation of the insured person.

This list is not comprehensive. Different insurance offices employ different criteria for assessing risks. It usually pays to obtain quotations from several companies as most of them attach different degrees of importance to the various factors, which can result in their quotations varying considerably in each case.

No-claims bonus

Motor insurance, like any kind of general insurance, lasts only one year, at the expiry of which it must be renewed. But with motor insurance there is usually a 'discount' on the amount of the renewal premium if no claim has been made under the policy in the previous year. This is designed to minimise trivial claims as well as to favour the careful driver, and is similar in effect to an 'excess' clause. For example, if your first year's premium is £100 and the no-claims discount on the first renewal premium is quoted as 25%, you are unlikely to make a claim under your policy if somebody does less than £25 worth of damage to your car. It would be cheaper to pay for the repair yourself – unless, of course, you have another accident in the following week!

The scale of no-claims bonuses varies but most insurers offer 25% for one claim-free year, rising successively to a maximum of 60% discount after four or five claim-free years. A single claim in, say, the sixth year will usually cause your no-claims bonus to fall back two years on the scale.

Other insurance

Insurance can usually be arranged, at a price, to indemnify you against losses arising from any reasonable hazards to yourself or your possessions.

Personal accident, often providing for the payment of stated amounts of compensation for specified injuries, is quite cheap, as the average risk to any one individual is small. Accident cover is often included in packaged insurance such as travel insurance.

Travel insurance. This insures against the usual risks associated with overseas travel, whether on business or holiday, such as medical treatment (for illness as well as accident), loss of luggage, tickets and cash (to a specified limit), and even the cancellation of the holiday or the failure of public transport. This is short-term insurance and premiums range from around £6 per week per person. Many tour organisations include travel insurance in the package.

Medical insurance, which secures hospital treatment as a private patient, is increasingly popular, although expensive. For an additional premium you can include costs of private consultations with a general practitioner, although the patient is usually required to pay for the first two or three consultations in a year (*i.e.* there is an 'excess').

Permanent health insurance is very different from medical insurance. This is a contract that provides for the payment of an agreed series of periodic payments to the insured should he become sick or disabled for a lengthy period and unable to carry on working. This insurance is not designed just to meet medical costs, but to provide an income to replace some of the income from employment which will cease or fall dramatically in the case of a long absence from work.

Life assurance

Whereas general or non-life insurance provides compensation in respect of a financial loss that may never arise, *life* insurance provides for specified cash payments to be made upon death – an event that is certain to take place sometime. The principle of indemnity is not present in life insurance. Instead of being insured *against* some event occurring, you are *assured* of the payment of a determinable amount of money being made to your dependants on the occurrence of a specified event. It is for this reason that one often speaks of life *assurance* rather than of life *insurance*.

Life premiums

Another important distinction between general insurance and life assurance is concerned with the calculation of premiums. General insurance against a risk is a short-term contract, generally for a maximum of one year. On its expiry the contract may be renewed, but the renewal premium may not be at the same rate as the original premium. It may be higher or lower according to how the underwriters reassess the risk.

Life assurance, however, is not an annual contract, but one either for your whole life or for an agreed period of years. It would be a contradiction in terms were an agreement to be made for an assured sum to be payable on death in exchange for an annual premium if that premium could be varied from year to year by the insurance company. Clearly as you grow older you are more likely to die, so the insurance company's risk becomes greater. You might, of course, pay a small premium as a young person and a successively higher premium as you get older or contract various illnesses, but this would be impracticable. The modern method is for the premium to be for a fixed annual amount for the whole period of the insurance such that it reflects the average risk over the whole term. It is thus more than adequate for covering the risk in the early years but less than adequate in later years.

Premiums for life assurance are, therefore, what are called 'level' premiums. They are calculated according to the assessed life expectancy of the assured person. Main factors affecting life expectancy include:

(*a*)   *sex* – the average woman lives four years longer than the average man;

(*b*)   *age at entry* – from past records it is known how many years a person of any age can expect to live, on average, and assuming no bad record of health;

(*c*)   *occupation* – life expectancy varies for different types of occupation;

(*d*)   *recreational activities* – certain pursuits are considered to be unduly hazardous, *e.g.* car racing, hang gliding, rock climbing;

(*e*)   *state of health* –not only your present condition but your record of health in the past is taken into consideration; mortality and illness record of your immediate kin are also relevant.

Whole-life assurance

Whole-life assurance is an agreement whereby the 'life office', as the insurance company is often called, undertakes to pay a predetermined sum of money called 'the sum assured' when you die. Premiums are usually payable throughout life, but they can be arranged to cease at age 60 or 65, in which case the annual premium would be a little higher. The life office knows from its records the average age at which people currently of your age die, and is almost making a bet with you that you will not meet with a premature end.

The purpose of whole-life assurance is to set up a fund for use on your death whether that occurs sooner or later. It is thus a convenient way of making provision for the widow of a man whose pension arrangements do not include widow's benefits. It can also be used for setting up a fund for paying capital transfer tax on the death of a fairly wealthy person, thus protecting the value of the inheritance. You yourself can never enjoy the benefits of whole-life assurance.

Term assurance

Purely as a protection for one's wife and family in the event of the premature death of the breadwinner, the cheapest kind of life assurance is what is called 'term cover'. The word 'term' simply signifies that the assurance lasts only for the duration of the selected term of years. It is much cheaper than whole-life assurance because you are much less likely to die during any stated number of years than you are to die some time.

A 30-year-old man can insure his life for £25,000 over a term of 20 years (long enough for the children to grow up) for around £4 gross per month.

Income benefit

A variation of term cover is insurance that will pay your dependants on your death an annual income for the remaining years of the chosen term, instead of paying a single lump sum. A Family Income Policy over 20 years to provide an income of £3,000 a year in the event of your death during that term would cost a 30-year old about £3 gross per month.

Mortgage protection

A particular form of term policy is one designed merely to pay off the outstanding debt on a repayment mortgage in the event of the death of the mortgagor. This is called a 'reducing term policy'. It costs in premium even less than ordinary level term because the insured amount falls in line with the reduction of the oustanding amount of the mortgage.

Endowment assurance

Endowment assurance, unlike simple term assurance, provides not only protection for your dependants in the event of your death during its term but also a profitable means of saving and investing for your own future. In exchange for the regular premiums the insurance company undertakes to pay the amount of the policy either to you personally at the end of the selected period, or to your estate should you die in the meantime.

For the younger person in first-class health the best kind of endowment policy is the 'with-profits' one. The claim value of this kind of policy is the original face value plus accrued 'profits' or bonuses that are declared annually (or at longer intervals) and which are added to the guaranteed amount which will be paid at the end of the endowment period or on prior death. Most with-profits policies also enjoy what is called a 'terminal' or 'claims' bonus – that is to say, when the policy becomes a claim, either on maturity or on prior death, the amount to be paid out consists not only of the original amount plus accumulated 'reversionary' bonuses to date, but also an additional final bonus determined by the then capital profits made by the insurance company on its investments. The terminal bonus is less accurately predictable than the regular or reversionary bonuses, so it should be looked on more as a windfall gain rather than as an anticipated investment yield.

Personal expenditure

Premiums on a with-profits policy are naturally higher than those on a without-profits policy but, pound for pound, they are usually a better buy from an investment point of view.

With-profits

Both whole-life and endowment policies can be arranged on a with-profits basis. When you obtain a quotation from an insurance company, the estimated maturity value will be based on the current bonus rates being declared and will project on this basis what the policy will be worth at the end of the period.

With a good life office the value in 25 years' time of a with-profits endowment policy could well exceed three times its original amount. But bonuses are not guaranteed until they have been declared, for the rates depend on profits yet to be earned.

Joint life assurance

It is common practice for a married couple to take out life assurance on each life. Often they choose an endowment policy on the life of the husband and a (much cheaper) term policy on the life of the wife. The purpose in insuring the life of the wife, even though she may not necessarily be earning an income, is to give financial protection to the husband should he be faced with the problem of bringing up a family single-handed and of having to employ a housekeeper.

Consideration should be given in such circumstances to an alternative and usually very much more economical way of providing this protection with *one* insurance policy. This takes the form of a single policy on *both lives jointly*, the benefits to be payable on the death of the first of them or, if an endowment policy, at the end of the agreed period. The premium on joint life assurance is only slightly higher than on a single life.

Tax relief

Premiums payable on life policies for terms of not less than 10 years are allowable for tax relief at 17.5% (reduced to 15% as from April 1981). There are certain restrictions and conditions on this relief but these are of little consequence to the average United Kingdom resident of modest means. There is no need to make any claim for the tax relief as the amount you actually pay to the life office as premium is not the full amount but the net amount after tax relief.

TEST QUESTIONS

1. Describe the basic purpose of general insurance.
2. On what basis is the premium payable for insurance calculated?
3. A claim made under an insurance contract is restricted to the amount of the financial loss actually suffered. What are the two terms used to describe this basic principle?
4. What is the fundamental difference between life and non-life insurance?
5. What is meant by a 'new-for-old' insurance contract?
6. Against what main hazards would you advise a home owner to insure?
7. What is the meaning of the term 'excess' in an insurance contract?
8. What do you understand by the term 'public liability'?
9. Premiums payable on renewal of a contract for general insurance may not be identical with the original premium. Suggest three reasons for this.
10. It is illegal to drive a motor vehicle on a public highway without stipulated minimum insurance. What is the minimum cover required by law?
11. What risks additional to those required by the law do most third-party insurance contracts include?
12. What do you understand by the term 'comprehensive cover' in the case of motor insurance?
13. Premiums for motor insurance vary very widely indeed. On what main bases do the underwriters assess the risks, and thus the premiums?
14. Describe the operation of the 'no-claims bonus' system.
15. Give examples of non-life insurance other than for buildings, house contents and motor car, that might be appropriate for private individuals in certain circumstances.
16. What is meant by the term 'level premiums' in connection with life assurance?
17. What five main considerations govern the scale of premiums for life assurance?
18. Define whole-life assurance. What are its main purposes?
19. What is term life assurance?
20. Term assurance can be arranged to provide benefits in the form of a regular income for dependants instead of a single capital sum. What is the name given to this form of cover?
21. Only one kind of life assurance can provide benefits that the insured person can live to enjoy. What is this? Describe how it works.
22. Explain the difference between annual reversionary bonuses and terminal bonuses.

EXERCISE

John Forbes, ages 23, has driven his father's car without incident for five years. He lives in Nottingham and contemplates buying his first car. He has obtained tariffs from two insurance companies for comprehensive cover and notices that the car he hopes to buy would be included in Group 4 of Company A and Group 2 of Company B.

Company A: premium rates per annum

Group	London postal area £	Major towns in UK £	Rest of UK £
1	150	130	100
2	200	160	120
3	250	200	150
4	400	350	250
5	500	400	300

Reductions are successively allowed for:

(*a*)	excluding drivers under 25	5%
(*b*)	accepting excess of £25 per claim	10%
(*c*)	no-claim bonuses: after first year	10%
	after 2nd year	25%
	after 3rd year	40%
	after 4th year	60%

Company B: premium rates per annum

Group	London metropolitan police area £	Rest of UK £
1	250	200
2	300	250
3	400	350
4	450	400

A surcharge of 20% is added to gross premiums for all sports cars. Subsequently, reductions are successively allowed for:

(*a*)	excluding drivers under 25	10%
(*b*)	accepting excess of £50 any claim	10%
(*c*)	no-claim bonuses: after 1st year	10%
	after 2nd year	25%
	after 3rd year	50%

Which company offers the lowest premium in the first year, assuming advantage is taken of all possible reductions?

Which company offers the lowest premium, after taking advantage of all possible reductions, in the fifth year, assuming John has had four years of no claims?

Explain why the figures are higher for the London area than elsewhere.

PART FIVE

Financial statements

13 Income and expenditure accounts and balance sheets

Personal accounts

It is a salutary exercise to work out your personal budget over a period of, say, a year. A budget is merely a list of all items of income to be received and cash to be paid – in other words, it is an estimate of what your receipts and payments account would look like at the end of a year. Planning a budget can be a very useful device for judging what you can and cannot afford to buy.

A young man or woman just starting work at 18 or 19 might rough out figures on the following lines. Although the figure for basic wages is reasonably accurate, since the starting wage is known to be £44 a week, the figure for overtime is an estimate based on what others in the same firm have said they are getting. Payments for National Insurance contributions, income tax PAYE deductions and company pension plan contributions are reasonably calculated at current (1980/81) rates. The remaining items of expenditure are estimates.

Preliminary budget for one year

Money paid out	£	Money received	£
NI contributions	144	Gross basic wages	2,288
Income tax	480	Estimated overtime	696
Company pension		Interest on £200 in	
contributions	108	building society	21
Board and lodging			
(living with			
parents)	540		
Fares to work	240		
Carried over	1,512		3,005

	£	£
Brought forward	1,512	3,005
Midday meals	180	
Clothes	300	
Holidays	120	
Saving £20 monthly in building society	240	
Spending money (say)	250	
	2,602	
Budgeted excess of income over spending	403	
	3,005	3,005

Let us assume that, after starting work, this person finds that some items of expenditure have been overestimated and others underestimated, but that on balance he still seems to be budgeting for a surplus of some £400. Assume that he decides to allocate some of this to an additional contractual savings plan of £10 a month in the index-linked National Savings, some to the purchase for cash of a transistor radio, and some to the purchase on HP of a motorbike.

At the end of 12 months he decides to prepare a proper account recording his actual performance regarding income and spending. He nets his wages (gross less deductions) and the take-home pay is easily worked out from his pay slips. Much of his expenditure is recorded in his bank statement and cheque counterfoils. He notices that his credit bank balance is £40 lower than it was at the beginning of the year. This is what his actual receipts and payments statement looks like.

Payments	£	*Receipts*	£
Board and lodging	624	Net wages	2,380
Fares to work	290	Building society	
Midday meals	200	interest	32
Clothing	210		
Holiday	160		
Bought motorbike on HP (8 monthly instalments of £40. Total cost £480)	320*		
Carried over	1,804		2,412

	£		£
Brought forward	1,804		2,412
Petrol, oil, licence repairs and insurance	130		
Bought radio	35*		
£20 monthly to building society	240*		
£10 monthly for 10 months index-linked savings	100*		
Identifiable payments	2,309		2,412

Now, in this list no account has been taken of everyday pocket money spending, since no record has been kept. On the face of it the above figures account for all income received except for £103 (£2,412 minus £2,309). But his bank balance has fallen by £40, so he concludes that he must have spent £103 plus £40 = £143 on unidentifiable items. This is represented by the two items below:

Spending money	143	Drawn from bank	40
	2,452		2,452

Assets and liabilities

Notice that some of the items of expenditure in the receipts and payments statement above (those marked *) are capital expenditure, not revenue expenditure, since they have resulted in the acquisition of capital assets (motorbike and radio), or of investments (payments to building society and index-linked SAYE). In properly constructed accounts such items would not have appeared in an income and expenditure account but in the balance sheet, which is a statement of all assets owned and liabilities owed. In this case the relevant balance sheet would look like the following, if we accept that the two capital assets purchased have lost value (depreciated) since their purchase by 20%. Relevant figures at the beginning of the year are shown in brackets for comparison.

Balance sheet at end of year

Liabilities	£	£		Assets		£	£	
HP debt				Motorbike at				
(4 × £40				cost	£480			
instal-				*less* Depreciation				
ments	160	(nil)		at 20%	£96	384	(nil)	
Capital account				Radio set at				
opening				cost	£35			
balance	£330							
add Excess of								
income over				*less* Depreciation	£7	28	(nil)	
revenue expen-				Building				
diture				society share				
£552	882	(330)		account		440	(200)	
	1,042			SAYE (index-linked)		100	(nil)	
				Balance at bank		90	(130)	
						1,042		

Now we must reconstruct the receipts and payments statement and present it in the proper form of an income and expenditure account. Capital spending has been removed, and a charge for depreciation introduced.

Income and expenditure account

Expenditure	£	Income	£
Board and lodging	624	Net take-home pay	2,380
Fares to work	290	Building society	
Midday meals	200	interest	32
Clothing	210		
Holiday	160		
Running expenses of			
motorbike	130		
Depreciation of			
assets	103		
Unidentified			
spending	143		
	1,860		
Balance, being			
excess of income			
over spending	552		
	2,412		2,412

Accounts of clubs and societies

The annual statement of the financial affairs of societies and other non-profit-making organisations takes a form very similar to that of the personal income and expenditure account and balance sheet described above. Exactly the same principles are followed of distinguishing between *capital* receipts and payments, which will be reflected in the statement of liabilities and assets (the balance sheet), and *revenue* receipts and expenditure which will form the basis of the income and expenditure account.

An added refinement is that, where revenue receipts and payments relate to a succeeding or preceding period to the one under review, they should be excluded, and suitable entries made in the balance sheet. Similarly, where amounts due to be received or paid in the current period are not so received or paid they should be included, and provision made in the balance sheet.

Example

The Gavin Sports Club was founded one year ago by a donation from Gavin Engineering Ltd of a cash sum of £5,000 and a wooden pavilion valued at £1,000, together with a 20-year lease of a playing field at an annual rental of £250. The following transactions took place in the following 12 months.

	£
Paid for construction of tennis court	1,020
Wages to part-time groundsman	1,200
Paid ground rent	375[1]
Bought furniture and fittings	1,400
Cost of printing, stationery, and postage	135[2]
Received subscriptions	1,400[3]
Received proceeds of concert	440
Transferred cash to bank deposit account	1,500
Earned interest on deposit account	230
Bought mowing equipment	470[4]

Notes:

1. This includes £125 ground rent for the succeeding year, paid in advance.
2. This includes £15 worth of headed paper held for stock.
3. Subscriptions due but not received amount to £328 and of course are not included in the £1,400.
4. Of the sum of £470 an amount of £127 is still owed to Garden Equipment Ltd for a small mower for which no account has yet been received.

Using the basic information given above, one can draw up an income

146

and expenditure account for the first year's operations, and a balance sheet showing the liabilities and assets at the end of that year, and this is shown overleaf. Depreciation has been written off at 10% a year on the value of the pavilion and tennis court, and at 20% on furniture, fittings and equipment.

Interpretation

A member of this club, on being presented with a copy of these accounts, can obtain a very comprehensive picture of how its financial affairs have been looked after.

On a current basis he will see that the club's expenditure has been £252 less than its revenue, including the writing down of wasting assets; so its capital has risen from the original grant of £5,000 and gift of pavilion of £1,000 (£6,000) to £6,252, which is very satisfactory.

The balance sheet shows how the capital has been disposed in acquiring useful assets suitable to the purpose of the club. Those that wear out or have a limited life have been appropriately written down, the depreciation being charged against revenue.

The cash position looks healthy as there is £1,097 in the current bank account and £1,500 on deposit, where it is earning interest. Presumably some of the money in current account is about to be used for acquiring further assets, since otherwise it would be better to put it on deposit account.

Less satisfactory is that £328 is outstanding on overdue subscriptions. The treasurer should be asked to chase these slow payers.

Small businesses

The same method of preparing final accounts is also suitable for businesses run by a sole proprietor, although if he is trading in commodities, or is a manufacturer, amounts must be shown for stocks of raw materials and partly finished and finished goods, and also for his purchases of goodwill where a going concern has been acquired by a purchaser at a price that includes an amount in respect of the 'goodwill' built up by the previous owner – in other words with the customer connection. A shop or guest house, for example, often changes hands at a figure above the value of net assets, reflecting the hard work the seller has put into building up the profitability of the business.

As a rough and ready guide, the value set on goodwill should be of such a figure as will, with the other net assets, come to a total purchase price for the business that will cause the annual net profits to represent a reasonable yield on the total cost, including goodwill. Should profits be only at a rate reflecting a fair return on the capital invested in real assets, then there is no goodwill.

In a business it is also prudent to make provisions for losses

GAVIN SPORTS CLUB ACCOUNTS (*see* Example on page 146)

Income and Expenditure Account

Expenditure	£	*Income*	£
Wages	1,200	Subscriptions	1,728
Ground rent	250	Concert proceeds	440
Printing, stationery, postage	120	Bank interest	230
Depreciation (100 + 102 + 280 + 94)	576		
	2,146		
Excess of income over expenditure to Capital Account	252		
	2,398		2,398

Balance Sheet as at (date)

Liabilities	£	£	*Assets*	£	£	£
Capital Account	6,000		*Fixed assets*			
Excess of income over expenditure for year	252	6,252	Pavilion at valuation		1,000	
			less Depreciation at 10%		100	900
Sundry creditors			Tennis court at cost		1,020	
Garden Equipment Ltd		127	*less* Depreciation at 10%		102	918
			Furniture and fittings at cost		1,400	
			less Depreciation at 20%		280	1,120
			Equipment at cost		470	
			less Depreciation at 20%		94	376
			Total fixed assets			3,314

(Balance Sheet cont'd)
Liabilities

	£		£	£
		Assets		
		Current assets		
		Cash in current account	1,097	
		Investment (on deposit)	1,500	
		Stationery stock	15	
		Ground rent in advance	125	
		Overdue subscriptions	328	
		Total current assets		3,065
	6,379			6,379

Note The figure for cash on current bank account is arrived at as follows.

	£			£
Money received		*Money paid out*		
Gavin Engineering	5,000	Tennis court construction		1,020
		Ground rent		375
Concert	440	Furniture and fittings		1,400
Interest	230	Printing and stationery, etc.		135
		Placed in deposit account		1,500
		Mowing equipment	£470	
		less not yet paid	£127	343
				(5,973)
		Thus, balance in bank		1,097
	7,070			7,070

deemed likely to arise. The commonest provision is one for bad or doubtful debts. Where there are very many credit customers, and where the total due from them is large, it is reasonable to assume that a small proportion of them will fail to pay. In this case an amount of, say, 2% to 5% of the total of debtors might be written off current profits and held in a 'provision' account. This can be topped up as total debtors rise, or written back to profits as total debtors fall.

'Reserves' are different from provisions. Making a provision is merely being cautious in not taking credit for profits which may not materialise; creating a reserve is an allocation of profits actually made to a special pool – this may be for some specific purpose, such as to meet costs of future new equipment, or just as a cushion for emergencies. In one-man business it is not usually considered necessary to create a 'general reserve', it being sufficient merely to place all undrawn profits into the proprietor's own capital account.

Example
Shown on pages 152–3 are the final accounts of a retail jeweller at the end of his financial year to 30 June 1980. You are required to make an assessment of his progress and comment on the accounts, interpreting them for a layman.

Interpretation
1. *Gross profit* is the amount by which total sales of goods (in this case) exceeds the cost of those goods. In a manufacturing industry costs would have included direct wages. The first item of expenditure shown in the account is arrived at by taking the value of stock of jewellery at the beginning of the year, adding the costs of goods purchased during the year, and deducting the value of the goods still in stock at the end of the year, valued at cost price. This will give the total cost of all items sold. Deducted from total sales turnover of £35,305 this indicates a gross trading profit of £13,920. To determine the percentage gross profit (*i.e.* rate of mark up) one divides the gross profit by the costs of sales (13,924 ÷ 21,385) and multiplies by 100 to give about 65%.

2. *Net profit* is the amount of profit left out of gross profit after all expenses have been deducted. The net profit is shown as £7,328. Now, the proprietor appeared to have £33,181 of his own capital invested in this business at the beginning of the year. Capital costs money, just as labour does. If he had had to borrow this amount of money at, say 15%, he would have had to pay interest on it of almost £5,000 a year. If he is using his own money then he is forfeiting the interest of £5,000 a year he would have received had he invested it in, say, gilt-edged securities. So it appears that his year's work in running this business has provided him with an income in terms of profit of only £2,328 more than he could have

earned doing nothing. In fact the net profit expressed as a percentage of proprietor's capital is only around 22%. As a percentage of total sales it is just over 20%.

3. *Rate of stock turnover.* Total goods sold in the year, valued at cost, stand at a figure below the average stock held. This indicates that goods are being turned over less than once a year. In other words, each item is, on average, held for more than a year before it is sold. There is something wrong here. It would be normal for stock to turn over about three to four times a year. Is some of the stock unsaleable?

4. *Fixed capital.* This is the term used to denote that part of the capital employed in a business that is tied up in fixed assets of a long-term nature, assets that cannot easily be sold or exchanged for others. This business has little in the way of fixed assets – only furniture and fittings valued at £1,710. Goodwill cannot easily be disposed of, but it is not a fixed asset except in a fictional sense; it is better to describe it, therefore as a fictitious asset.

5. *Working capital.* This is the term used to describe that part of business capital which is continually circulating between cash, goods, debtors and creditors; in other words, it is the trading capital. The quantity of working capital can be calculated from a balance sheet by adding together all the *current assets* – in this case Stock £36,827, Debtors £4,193, and Balance at bank £2,191 plus Expenses paid in advance £184 (total £43,396), and deducting the *current liabilities* of Creditors £13,547 and £250 (13,797), making a figure of £29,599. Current assets less current liabilities gives a figure sometimes referred to as *net current assets*, but more generally known as working capital. On the balance sheet figures in the case of the business under review, working capital is more than adequate. The suspicious feature in this case is the very large proportion of this that consists of stock. Much of the stock carried is being financed by trade creditors – in other words, it hasn't been paid for.

6. *Credit taken.* Balance sheet figure for trade creditors is nearly half as much as total purchases for the year. One should suspect the business of being saddled with stock it can't sell (*see* 3 above), and of consequently being unable to pay its bills. Note that the *liquid assets* (cash and near cash) of Bank balance and Debtors is less than half the amount owed to Creditors. If the creditors were to press for payment the business might be forced into liquidation, stock having to be sold off at give-away prices.

7. *Credit given.* Sundry debtors at £4,193 are the customers to whom he has sold goods on credit, and who have not yet paid their bills. As a proportion of total sales this looks reasonable, but without knowing what total credit sales were (jewellers sell mostly for cash) one cannot make a reasonable judgement on this.

RETAIL JEWELLER'S ACCOUNTS to 30 June 1980 (*see* Example on page 150)

Income and Expenditure Account

Expenditure	£	£	*Income*	£
Cost of goods sold			Total sales	35,305
Opening stock	32,856		Repair work	406
Purchases	25,356			
	58,212			
Closing stock	36,827			
Cost price of sales		21,385		
Wages and salaries		3,323		
Rent and rates		1,675		
Heat, light, insurance		374		
Carriage on goods		77		
Advertising		316		
Stationery and telephone		142		
Discounts given		53		
Sundry expenses		568		
Bad debt written off		280		
Depreciation		190		
		28,383		
Net profit to Capital Account		7,328		
		35,711		35,711

Balance Sheet as at 30 June 1980

Liabilities	£	£	£
Capital Account			
as at start		33,181	
Net profit		7,328	
		40,509	
less Drawings		4,500	
		36,009	
less:			
Write-off			
Goodwill	950		
Provision for doubtful debts	210	1,160	
			34,849
Provision for doubtful debts			210
Trade creditors			13,547
Rent due but unpaid			250
			48,856

Assets	£	£
Fixtures and Fittings		
as at valuation	1,900	
less 10% depreciation	190	1,710
Stock in hand		36,827
Sundry debtors		4,193
Balance at bank		2,192
Rates paid in advance		184
		45,106
Goodwill as at start of year	4,700	
less 20% written off	950	3,750
		48,856

8. *Reserves and provisions.*

(a)   Depreciation of 10% has been written off fixtures and fittings and is charged in the income and expenditure account.

(b)   Bad debts of £280 have also been charged against profits, the jeweller evidently being satisfied that this amount cannot be recovered. Two other items of a provision nature appear in the balance sheet but do not figure in the income and expenditure account – namely Provision for doubtful debts £210 and write-off of part (20%) of goodwill (£950). Instead of being treated as expenses of the business these are treated as allocations of profits and thus are shown as deductions from proprietor's capital *after* the net profit has been added to it. This is perfectly in order, although not the usual accepted procedure. Presumably the proprietor originally bought the ingoing of the shop at some thousands of pounds more than the value of net assets, and is writing this off at 20% each year worked on the reducing balance. In the course of a few years he will be able to eliminate this item from the balance sheet. Indeed, it seems questionable whether this business has any goodwill value at all.

9. *Drawings.* The proprietor has drawn out of the business a sum of £4,500 as his remuneration for the year. His own capital account is thus shown as £1,668 higher than it was at the beginning of the year (£34,849 minus £33,181).

Profit and loss account

For a small non-trading business, such as that of a self-employed architect, solicitor, designer or consultant, it is perfectly satisfactory for all items of current income and revenue expenditure to be presented in the form of a Revenue and Expenditure Account. In the case of a merchant or any large scale trader in commodities it is preferable for purposes of presentation to marshall the buying and selling items in a separate preliminary account called the Trading Account. Other items, representing indirect costs or 'overheads', are accommodated in a Profit and Loss Account.

Trading Account

The debit or left-hand side of the Trading Account will contain:

(a)   commencing stock;

(b)   purchase of goods or materials;

(c)   wages and any other expenditure deemed to be directly connected with the creation of the sales.

On the credit side will be placed the total sales for the period, and the value of the closing stock. Total debits should come to less than total credits, and the differences represents gross profit on trading.

This amount will be entered as the final item on the debit side to cause the two sides to balance, and will be carried down as 'gross profit' to the credit side of the Profit and Loss Account.

Profit and Loss Account

The Profit and Loss Account then starts off with the gross trading profit on the right-hand side. The business may have other items of revenue, such as interest on money invested. If so, these items will also appear on the right-hand side.

Manufacturing Account

For a business that is engaged in manufacturing as well as distributing, a further division of expenditure is sometimes made so that all the costs of materials, direct manufacturing wages and other expenditure directly connected with the *manufacture* are marshalled in a Manufacturing Account, the balance representing the cost of actual manufacture being carried down to a Trading Account or, if no retail sales are made, directly to the Profit and Loss Account. Unless a business engages in both manufacture *and* trading in a big way, there may be no need for *both* Manufacturing *and* Trading Account.

Example

The following balances were extracted from the books of Andrew Shelton, a toy manufacturer, at the close of his year, 31 December 1979:

Trial Balance

		Debits £		Credits £
Capital account				90,000
Drawings Account		7,000		
Purchases	T	47,970		
Sales	T		T	148,020
Commencing stock	T	11,460		
Salaries	P	6,280		
Manufacturing wages	T	38,560		
Leasehold factory		25,000		
Rent, rates and insurance	P	6,940		
Office expenses	P	9,520		
Plant and machinery		24,000		
Provision for bad debts as at 1 Jan. 79				3,240
Factory fuel consumed	T	7,950		
Sundry debtors		40,210		
Sundry creditors				16,980
Carried over		224,890		258,240

155

Financial statements

	£	£
Brought forward	224,890	258,240
Cash at bank	17,770	
Cash in hand	2,210	
Office furniture	3,500	
Salesmen's wages and commission P	9,870	
	258,240	258,240

Prepare a Trading Account (no separate Manufacturing Account) and Profit and Loss Account for the year ended 31 December 1979. Before closing the account make necessary adjustments for the following:

1. Depreciation is to be written off assets as follows:
   Premises   5% per annum
   Plant and machinery   10% per annum
   Office furniture   10% per annum.
2. The 'provision for bad debts' is to be increased to £4,000.
3. Value of closing stock is £14,290.
4. Wages of £570 have been earned and are accrued due but unpaid as at 31st December.

What is the net profit as a percentage of sales?
What is the net profit as a percentage of capital employed?
What is the rate of turnover of stock?
What is Andrew Shelton's working capital?

Answer: The way to tackle this is first to mark the items in the Trial Balance that are to appear in the Trading Account (marked T above), and in the Profit and Loss Account (marked P). The remaining items, being assets or liabilities and not items of income or expenditure, are to appear in the balance sheet.

To construct the Trading Account, transfer the items marked T to the same side of the Trading Account as they appear in the Trial Balance. Consider which of the required adjustments have to be made in this account. Wages accrued but unpaid of £570 must be added to the wages figure and also treated as a provision on the liabilities side of the balance sheet. It is also clear that depreciation of plant and machinery is a direct trading (or manufacturing) cost, so 10% of the value must appear as an expenditure in the Trading Account, and the amount deducted from the asset value of machinery when we come to prepare the balance sheet. Tot up the two sides of the Trading Account and you find you have to add £53,400 to the debit side to make the account balance. Bring this gross profit down to the credit side of the Profit and Loss Account.

To construct the Profit and Loss Account, deal with items marked P in a similar way, writing off depreciation at the prescribed rates from furniture and premises (remembering to adjust the asset values for the Balance Sheet). A further debit entry of £760 must be created for 'Provision for bad debts', and that amount added to the existing provision as a liability in the Balance Sheet. The balance remaining in the Profit and Loss Account is transferred to Capital Account (or Drawings a/c).

Balances remaining are all items for the Balance Sheet. The following adjustments have to be made:

(*a*)	to Capital Account	add the net profit
		deduct drawings
(*b*)	to Premises, Plant and machinery, and Office furniture	deduct depreciation
(*c*)	to Debtors	deduct the new total for Provision for Bad Debts (now £4,000). Alternatively, this provision could be shown as a liability in the Balance Sheet
(*d*)	Provision for wages accrued due	create a provision (a liability) of £570

Trading Account *for year to 31 December 1979*

Debit		£	Credit	£
Opening stock		11,460	Sales	148,020
Purchases		47,970	Closing stock	14,290
Manufacturing wages	£38,560			
	570	39,130		
Factory fuel		7,950		
Depreciation of plant, etc.		2,400		
Gross trading profit		53,400		
		162,310		162,310

Profit and Loss Account

Debit	£	Credit	£
Salaries	6,280	Gross profit	53,400
Rent, rates, & insurance	6,940		
Salesmen's salaries and commission	9,870		
Office expenses	9,520		
Provision for bad debts	760		
Carried over	33,370		53,400

Financial statements

	£		£
Brought forward		33,370	53,400
Depreciation:			
leasehold	1,250		
furniture	350	1,600	
Net profit		18,430	
		53,400	53,400

Balance sheet *at 31 December 1979*

Liabilities	£	£	Assets	£	£
Capital Account			Leasehold premises		
at 1 Jan. 1979	90,000		at 1 Jan. 1979	25,000	
Net profit	18,430		Depreciation	1,250	23,750
	108,430				
less Drawings	7,000	101,430	Plant and machinery		
			at 1 Jan. 1979	24,000	
			Depreciation	2,400	21,600
Sundry creditors		16,980	Office furniture		
Provision for accrued		570	at 1 Jan. 1979	3,500	
wages			Depreciation	350	3,150
			Stock		14,290
			Sundry debtors	40,210	
			less Provision for bad		
			debts	4,000	36,210
			Balance at bank		17,770
			Cash in hand		2,210
		118,980			118,980

Percentage net profit to sales = 18,430 : 148,020 = 12.5%

Net profit as percentage of capital employed = 18,430 : 101,430 = 18.2%

Rate of stock turnover = average stock is

$$\frac{11,460 + 14,290}{2}$$

= 12,870 : 148,020 = 11 times
(If this were calculated on *cost* of sales, instead of sales, the formula would be:

$$
\begin{aligned}
12,870 :\quad & 11,460 \\
+\ & 47,970 \\
\hline
& 59,430 \\
-\ & 14,290 = 45,140 \\
\hline
& = 3\frac{1}{2}\ \text{times}
\end{aligned}
$$

This is a more meaningful ratio.)

Working capital = 14,290 + 36,210 + 17,770 + 2,210
− 16,980 = £53,500

The business seems perfectly viable, but net profit to sales and to capital employed is on the low side. Salaries, salesmen's remuneration and office expenses amount to £25,670, nearly half as much again as the net profit. Is there waste here?

Profitability and break-even point

The costs of any business can be broadly divided into fixed costs (sometimes called indirect costs because they are not directly related to the rate of business activity), and variable costs (or direct costs, because they vary more or less directly with turnover). These terms were described more fully in Chapter 9. Certain minimum fixed costs will be incurred even when turnover is nil. It follows that there must be a minimum volume of sales below which the business is bound to function at a loss. The level of activity at which net loss turns into net profit is called the 'break-even' point.

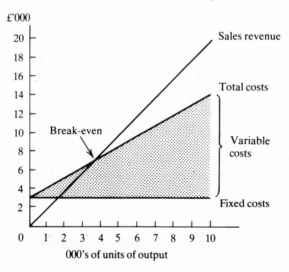

Fig. 13.1

In Fig. 13.1 the fixed costs up to a turnover of 10,000 units is £3,000. Over the whole of this range of turnover the *total* costs (fixed plus variable) rise from £3,000 at nil turnover to £14,000 at 10,000 turnover. The variable costs are represented by the

159

shaded area, and can be measured off by the height by which total costs exceed fixed costs at each point in the graph. Total revenue from sales is shown by the line at 45° to both axes, indicating that, in this instance, the selling price is fixed at £2 per unit sold. At levels of activity where total revenue falls short of total costs, the business makes a loss. The point where the revenue line cuts the total costs line is the break-even point because at this level of activity costs are just covered by revenue. So long as lines of total costs and total revenue retain their present straight-line shape the business will become more and more profitable as it expands, since some costs (fixed) do not rise, and are therefore spread over a larger turnover.

Unfortunately, these lines are liable to change their shape – they are not necessarily straight lines at all levels of activity. There is always a limit beyond which a business cannot be expanded without requiring a rise in fixed costs (such as the acquisition of an extra shop or factory or machine). Moreover, there is usually a point beyond which the variable costs cease to be strictly proportionate to sales, either (a) because it ceases to be possible to control the larger undertaking efficiently, or because of the need to employ less trained labour, or the need to pay overtime, or (b) because the larger turnover makes it possible to make economies in production, in which case variable costs would fall. In such cases the lines cease to be straight.

In Fig. 13.2 there is a sharp jump in fixed costs between outputs 5,000 and 6,000, possibly caused by the need to pay interest on additional capital, or the installation of an extra machine. Notice that total costs appear as a wavy line. Up to an output of 4,000 units they have been rising less than proportionately to turnover, indicating that variable costs per unit were falling. Between 4,000 and 6,000 units variable costs were proportionate to output, but above that level they were rising at an uneven pace. The most profitable output appears to be 11,000, at which point the total revenue line is at the highest level above total costs line.

It does not necessarily follow that the business should contract from an output of 13,000 to 11,000, but it does mean that the causes of the rise in variable costs should be looked into.

These comments are only by way of illustration of the fact that net profit does not necessarily vary proportionately with sales. As it is the general aim of every business to operate on such a scale as will create the maximum profit it is useful to calculate, for various levels of activity, the percentage rate of net profits to sales.

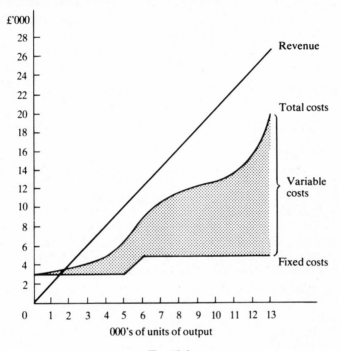

Fig. 13.2

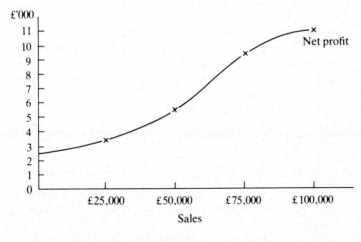

Fig. 13.3

Financial statements

In Fig. 13.3 the most profitable output appears to be £100,000, but as the curve is tending to the horizontal at that point it would appear to be inadvisable to expand output beyond this figure. The ratio of profit to sales is at a maximum when output is £75,000 (12.6%), beyond which the ratio falls to 11% at £100,000.

TEST QUESTIONS

1. Why are all receipts and payments of a capital nature excluded from an income and expenditure account?
2. A depreciation charge is treated as expenditure in an income and expenditure account, although it represents no movement in cash and is not included in the cash book. What is depreciation? On what sort of assets is it properly chargeable?
3. What is a balance sheet?
4. How would you account for expenses paid in advance (a) in the balance sheet, and (b) in the income and expenditure account?
5. How would you account for expenses incurred but not paid during the period (a) in the income and expenditure account and (b) in the balance sheet?
6. Why does a balance sheet always balance?
7. In the income and expenditure account (or the trading and profit and loss account), how is the *cost* of materials and goods sold calculated?
8. What do you understand by the term 'goodwill'?
9. How would you deal with a debt due to you from a person you know to be bankrupt and without means?
10. How would you show in the accounts that some of the debts due to you might turn out to be bad, but you don't know which?
11. What do you understand by a 'reserve'?
12. Define gross profit in the case of a manufacturing firm.
13. Define net profit.
14. What is meant by the 'rate of stock turnover'?
15. Distinguish between fixed assets and current assets.
16. What is the term used to describe the total of current assets less the total of current liabilities?
17. What are 'liquid assets'?
18. What is a 'break-even' point?
19. Describe the use made of the ratio that net profit bears to total sales in studying the performance of a business at various levels of activity.
20. What do you understand by the term 'percentage net profit to capital employed'?

162

EXERCISES

A   The cash and bank account of A. White, an ironmonger, show the following total entries during the year to 31 December 1980.

	£
Repairs to premises	1,500
Repairs to plant and machinery	2,500
Rates	2,900
Purchases	143,500
Sales	175,261
Sundry expenses	3,525
Wages	27,500
Salaries	7,250

The balance of cash in the bank is £8,725, and cash in the office till is £466. Stock is held valued at cost at £84,400. A total of £27,255 is owed to the business by debtors, and the business owes £22,500 to its creditors.

At the beginning of the year no cash was held in the till, stock was valued at £41,000, plant and machinery at £20,000, leasehold premises at £12,500, and office furniture at £920.

Draw up the income and expenditure account in such a way as to show, in the form of a sub-account, the gross profit – treating for this purpose the following expenditure as direct: wages; repairs to plant and machinery. Write off 15% depreciation on plant and machinery, 10% of leasehold premises, and 10% of furniture.

Calculate the rate of mark-up of gross profit, expressed as a percentage of *cost price of sales,* the percentage net profit of sales, and the percentage net profit to capital employed. What is the amount of working capital?

B

(*a*)   Prepare a balance sheet from the following information taken from the books of J. Jones at the end of his first year of trading on 30 November 1980:

	£		£
Freehold shop	25,000	Shop furniture and fittings at	
Stock	12,000	valuation	3,500
Cash at bank	5,800	Net profit for year	8,200
Amount owed to business		Wages owing to staff	320
by customers	6,800	Drawings in cash for	
Amount owed by		personal use	4,500
business	5,000		
Cash in hand	120		

(*b*)   Calculate J. Jones's working capital.

(*c*)   Jones contemplates installing a new shop front and display cases at a cost of £11,000, borrowing the money from the bank on the security of the shop. What effect would this have on his working capital?

(*d*)   Jones can perfectly well continue to trade without the extra work on the shop premises. What factors should he take into consideration in deciding whether to go ahead?

C   The graph in Fig. 13.4 illustrates the performance of a business in each of four years.

1.   In which year did the business make the most net profit?
2.   In which year was the percentage net profit to sales at the maximum?

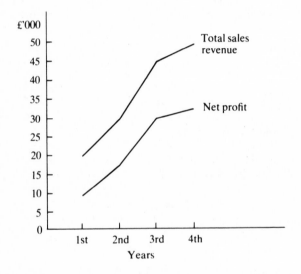

Fig. 13.4

14 How to read a company balance sheet

From the simple accounts of a small trader to the published accounts of public limited companies is quite a small step. The principles concerned are exactly the same, but what we have come to know as the income and expenditure account now takes the form of a profit and loss account. Moreover, this profit and loss account is usually divided into two parts – the first part, accommodating the proceeds of sales and the direct costs of producing the output, is called the trading account, the balancing item on which will be the gross profit; the second part, the profit and loss account proper, takes the gross profit from the trading account as the starting-off point, adding to that the receipts of income other than from sales (such as from investments) and accommodates all the indirect or overhead costs.

Single column final accounts

As for actual layout on the published page the final accounts of companies often take exactly the same form as was described in Chapter 13. But public companies are increasingly publishing their accounts in single column form, deducting the costs from profits, and deducting liabilities from assets. It is claimed that these are more readily understood by the layman, but presentation does not affect the figures in any way. To give the reader experience in recognising the alternative presentation the following example of a summarised and simplified balance sheet and profit and loss statement of a public company is provided in columnar form overleaf.

Having studied Chapter 6, most readers will have no difficulty in understanding the significance of most of the figures given. The only entries in this example that may not be readily comprehended are contained in the profit allocation at the end of the profit and loss statement.

(a)   *Provision for taxation* is the amount set aside out of current profits to meet the future demands of the taxman by way of corporation tax. From the fact that the liability for tax shown in the balance sheet is the same as the amount provided from current profits one deduces that there is no outstanding provision for future liability. Sophisticated students of accountancy will realise that this cannot be true, but this pretence makes it simpler to understand for the non-tax specialist.

A Processing Co. Ltd

Trading Account *for the year to 31 December, 1980*

	£	£
Total sales for the year		580,000
Materials consumed		
Commencing stock at 1 Jan	105,300	
add Purchases for year	460,000	
	565,300	
less Stock remaining 31 Dec	88,000	
Thus cost of material used in sales	477,300	
Wages paid	15,300	
Other processing costs	10,400	
Total processing costs of goods sold		503,000
Gross profit transferred to Profit and Loss Account		77,000

Profit and Loss Account *for the year to 31 December, 1980*

	£
Gross profit for year	77,000
Expenses: depreciation, staff salaries, heating, lighting, postage, telephone, carriage, administrative and selling costs, and directors' renumeration	25,500
Net profit before tax	51,500
Allocated as follows:	
Provision for taxation	24,000
Provision for net dividend (no interim dividend paid)	10,410
Transfer to Revenue Reserve	17,090
	51,500

Balance Sheet *as at 31 December, 1980*

Assets	£	£	£
Freehold premises			36,900
Plant and machinery			43,100
Total fixed assets			80,000
Stock in hand		88,000	
Trade debtors		65,200	
Liquid assets:			
Short-term deposits	28,000		
Cash at bank	28,300	56,300	
Total current assets			209,500
Total assets			289,500
less *Liabilities*			
Trade creditors		36,000	
Provision for dividend		10,410	
Provision for taxation		24,000	
Total outside liabilities (all current)			70,410
			219,090
Represented by:			
Issued ordinary share capital			100,000
(100,000 ordinary £1 shares)			
Revenue reserve			119,090
			219,090

(b)   *Provision for dividend* is the net amount of dividend recommended for payment to shareholders, but not yet paid.

(c)   *Transfer to reserves* is the amount left over from current profits but being retained in the business. It represents the amount by which the net value of the shareholders' stake has increased over the year, in money terms.

Interpretation

One can learn a great deal about a company from a study of the final accounts. The features one would select for particular attention will depend on whether the results are being analysed by an investor in the company (in which case *see* Chapter 6), a potential supplier of goods on credit to the company, a prospective employee of the company, or a lending banker.

An important factor concerning the performance and stability of the company, not normally revealed in a balance sheet, is the accuracy of the valuation of fixed assets and of stock. The basis of valuation is usually shown (*e.g.* historic cost less depreciation, or current replacement cost), but there is no way in which an outsider can check how realistic the basis is in practice.

In evaluating a company's financial statements it is the *proportions* of certain figures to each other rather than their absolute magnitudes that matter. These are expressed as ratios, often as percentage ratios. The main ratios are described below.

Solvency ratios

A would-be creditor of the company would seek to know whether, in the reasonably short term, all the outstanding liabilities of the company could be paid off without harming the company by having to dispose of productive assets. Three ratios used for this purpose (figures in brackets refer to the above example) are as follows.

Current ratio: current assets   : current liabilities
                         (209.5)   :   (70.4)   (= 3.0)
Liquid ratio: liquid assets   : current liabilities
                         (56.3)   :   (70.4)   (= 0.8)
Quick ratio: *(colloquially called the 'acid test')*
current assets *minus* the stock
(or liquid assets *plus* debtors)   : current liabilities
                         (121.5)   :   (70.4)   (= 1.7)

In our example it is quite clear from the first two ratios that there is no doubt about the current solvency of this company, since the outside liabilities can be paid off three times over from current assets, and that they could almost be paid out of cash. But with a balance sheet showing a less liquid position many analysts would apply the third ratio (the 'acid test'); this is considered to be more reliable since it excludes stock in hand which might, in the event, prove difficult to realise on a forced sale.

Operating ratios

Then comes the question of how efficiently the company is being run. Many indicators are available for this purpose and the following represent only the main ones used by most analysts. First we must define some new terms.

Shareholders' funds refers to the total nominal value of the issued ordinary shares, plus the reserves.
Capital employed refers to the total capital being used in the business, irrespective of who owns it. It therefore includes not only the total of ordinary shareholders' funds plus issued preference shares

and debentures, if any, but also capital borrowed from any source, including money by way of loan or overdraft from the bank. Capital employed is virtually the total assets in the balance sheet less the current trade creditors and any other (non-financing) outside creditors (*e.g.* Inland Revenue).

Current assets are those which, by their nature, are continuously changing from cash to stock to debtors and back to stock.

Current liabilities are those that will have to be paid off soon.

Working capital is the term used to described the excess of current assets over current liabilities (excluding liability to the bank, if any).

Now we come to the indicators. The figures in brackets again refer to the example on pages 167–168.

Current assets turnover:

sales	:	current assets	
(580,000)	:	(209,500)	(= 2.8)

This indicates that the current assets, whose nature it is to change form, are revolving nearly three times a year, which is rapid.

Stock turnover:

cost of stock sold	:	stock held	
(477,300)	:	(88,000)	(= 5.4)

This indicates a rapid movement. Stock is being turned over nearly six times a year, the average time any item is held in stock being just over two months. Compare this with the stock of the jeweller in Chapter 13. An analyst, however, would seek to find out why the stock held at 31 December is £17,300 lower than at the start of the year. This does call for an explanation (*see* 'working capital ratio' below).

Working capital turnover:

working capital	:	sales	
(139,090)	:	(580,000)	(= 24%)

This indicates that, provided no capital is lying idle, each £100 of sales is requiring working capital finance of £24 (but query: working capital figure includes £28,000 cash on short-term deposit – in other words this is *not* used for financing sales. Is this cash intended to be spent on purchasing larger stocks to meet expanding turnover in the next few months? If so, this might explain the reservation expressed above regarding low stock values at 31 December.)

Debtors turnover:

sales	:	debtors	
(580,000)	:	(65,200)	(= 9)

This shows that little over a month's credit is being taken by customers, who are clearly paying their bills promptly (assuming all customers are credit ones).

Mark-up:

gross profit	:	cost of sales	
(77,000)	:	(503,000)	(= 15%)

Net profit ratio:

net profit	:	sales	
(57,000)	:	(580,000)	(= 8.9%)

For a processing company, not a retail distributing one, this is a satisfactory result.

Gross return on capital employed:

gross trading profit	:	total capital employed	
(77,000)	:	(219,090)	(= 35%)

Net return on capital employed:

net profit	:	total capital employed	
(51,500)	:	(219,090)	(= 23.5%)

Both these ratios indicate great efficiency.

Net profit on working capital:

net profit	:	working capital	
(51,500)	:	(139,090)	(= 37%)

This indicates a very satisfactory use of working capital.

For other ratios, mainly of interest to shareholders, refer to Chapter 6.

Accounts of public companies

All limited companies prepare their final accounts more or less on the lines already described in this chapter, but the detailed figures are usually confidential within the company. Companies are not obliged to show all detail in their published accounts and it is usual for them to refrain from disclosing information they believe might be of use to their competitors and therefore damaging to the company, unless the law requires them to do so.

Thus it is very unusual for a public company to publish figures of their detailed costs – for example, it is normal for purchases, wages, and other direct costs to be lumped together in one sum. It follows that it is often impossible to calculate all the operating ratios described in the preceding section of this chapter. However, in the case of public quoted companies certain minimum information is required by law to be disclosed, either in the accounts themselves or by way of notes accompanying the accounts. The published Profit and Loss Account for the year ended 29 October 1978 of the Donald Macpherson Group Ltd, manufacturers of the popular 'Cover-Plus' household paint, is typical of the better-presented simplified accounts and is analysed below. Figures in italics are those for the previous year, included for comparison.

Consolidated Profit and Loss Account, Donald Macpherson Group Ltd
Year to 29 October 1978

	1978	1977
	£000	*£000*
Sales	65,490	*55,728*
Trading profiit	4,760	*3,877*
less Interest paid on loans and 7¼% loan stock (*less* Interest earned)	677	*837*
	4,083	*3,040*
Taxation	724	*1,377*
Profit after tax	3,359	*1,663*
Minority interest	2	*20*
Profit attributable to ordinary shareholders	3,357	*1,643*
(*add* Special item in 1977 only)		*+3*
Dividends paid and proposed	426	*376*
Transferred to Reserves	2,931	*1,270*

That was all. There was no Trading and Profit and Loss Account such as has been described in the preceding section of this chapter. But copious notes accompanied the above accounts amplifying and explaining the figures for the benefit of those who required more than the bare bones. From these notes one can partly reconstruct an account on the traditional lines as follows:

Trading Account *to 29 October 1978*
(Note that many items normally apearing in a Profit and Loss Account are shown in this Trading Account. It is not always possible to adhere to a precise pattern).

Debit	£000	£000	Credit	£000
Opening stock		11,443	Sales	65,490
All costs, including purchases, wages, salaries, and others except as below		62,067	Closing stock	14,658
Disclosed expenses				
Depreciation	686			
Vehicle leasing and contract hire	578			
Hire of plant and machinery	381			
Directors' emoluments	154			
Auditors' remuneration	79	1,878		
Trading profit		4,760		
		80,148		80,148

If we now carry the trading profit down we can reconstruct a traditional Profit and Loss Account, although it must be pointed out that it is not possible to distinguish between direct and indirect costs – in other words, all indirect costs or 'overheads' are included in the Trading Account.

Profit and Loss Account *to 29 October 1978*

		1978	1977
		£000	£000
Trading profit		4,760	3,877
Interest received on deposits		4	
		4,764	
Deduct			
Interest paid			*(Netted)*
on 7¼% loan stock	64		
on other short-term loans	617	681	837
Net profit before tax		4,083	3,040
Profit Allocation			
Taxation		724	1,377
Minority interests		2	20
Extraordinary item			3
Dividends paid and proposed		426	376
Transferred to Reserves		2,931	1,270
		4,083	3,040

The published Balance Sheet of the Donald Macpherson Group Ltd. took the form of a simplified single column, again supplemented by copious notes and comparative figures for the preceding year.

Balance Sheet, Donald Macpherson Group Ltd *as at 29 October 1978*

	£000	1978 £000	1977 £000
Fixed assets		9,144	8,751
Current assets			
Stocks	14,658		11,443
Quoted investments	1		
Trade and other debtors	14,963		13,168
Cash in hand and at bank	135	29,757	55
		38,901	33,417
Deduct:			
Current liabilities			
Bank overdraft and loans and acceptances	2,514		3,102
Creditors	12,456		8,949
Taxation	1,350		1,339
Proposed dividend	245	16,565	241
		22,336	19,786
Financed as follows:			
Shareholders' funds			
14,488,094 ord. 25p shares		3,622	3,570
Share premium account		450	294
Reserves		14,960	12,034
		19,032	15,898
Minority interests		50	109
7¼% loan stock		893	1,104
Medium-term loans		2,361	2,675
		22,336	19,786

The minority interests need not concern us. The Share Premium Account is a reserve created in the past by issues of ordinary shares at a subscription price above par.

Interpretation. Many, but not all, of the ratios described in the previous section of this chapter may be calculated from the above figures.

Working capital (or net current assets) is 29,757 *less* 16, 565, which comes to 13,192. Therefore:

Current ratio	is 29,757 : 16,565	=	1.8
Quick ratio	is 15,099 : 16,565	=	0.91
Current assets turnover	is 65,490 : 29,757	=	2.2 times

Stock turnover (taking the stock as the average of opening and closing stock, a half of 11,443 + 14,658) is

$$65,490 : 13,050 \qquad = \quad 5 \text{ times}$$

Financial statements

Debtors turnover   is 65,490 : 14,963   = 4.4 times
Net profit ratio before tax is
                           4,760 : 65,490   = 7.3%
Net return on capital employed (taking the employed capital as total assets less creditors, taxation, and dividend) is
                           4,764 : 23,869 (average of two years)
                                               = 19.95%

Net profit on working capital is
                           4,764 : 13,192   = 36.1%
Dividend per share is   426 : 14,488   = 2.9p net (equivalent
                                                  to 4.39p gross
                                                  of 33% tax, that
                                                  being the standard
                                                  rate in 1978/79)
Earnings per share are   3,357 : 14,488   = 23.2p net (equivalent
                                                  to 34.6p gross)

Notes: (*a*) The fact that new shares were issued during the year has been ignored for the sake of simplicity. (*b*) The company points out that had the full amount of deferred tax been charged against profits currently earned, earnings per share would have worked out at 12.9p net. This need not concern the non-specialist.)
Times dividend covered is   23.2 : 2.9   = 8 times

TEST QUESTIONS
1. What does the balancing item in a trading account represent?
2. In a trading and profit and loss account, where do the overhead expenses appear?
3. What ratios would you calculate in order to determine the degree of solvency of a company?
4. What do you understand by the term 'capital employed in the business'?
5. What ratio indicates the period that stock is, on average, being held before it is sold?
6. How would you assess whether customers are paying their bills promptly?
7. What ratio indicates percentage mark-up on purchases? 'Mark-up' is appropriate as an indicator only in certain kinds of undertakings. What undertakings are these?
8. What ratios in particular indicate the efficiency of a company in making profits?

EXERCISES
A From the figures reproduced on pages 175–176, and bearing in mind that the company is in the manufacturing business, calculate and comment on the following ratios.

(a)   Percentage gross profit to cost of sales (mark-up).
(b)   Percentage gross profit to sales.
(c)   Percentage net profit to sales.
(d)   Net return on capital employed.
(e)   Current ratio.
(f)   Liquid ratio.
(g)   Quick ratio (acid test).
(h)   Stock turnover.
(i)   Debtors turnover.
(j)   Working capital turnover.

A Manufacturing Co. Ltd

Profit and Loss Account *for year ending 31 December, 1980*

		£	£
Total sales			4,000,000
Cost of sales			
Opening stock of materials		170,000	
Purchases		1,320,000	
		1,490,000	
less Closing stock		235,000	
		1,255,000	
Manufacturing wages	£2,000,000		
Maintenance of machinery	£90,000	2,090,000	3,345,000
Gross profit			655,000
less Expenses			
Bank interest		125,000	
All other expenses including directors' remuneration		375,000	500,000
Net profit before tax			155,000
Allocated as follows:			
Provision for taxation		80,600	
Provision for dividend		34,000	
Transfer to Reserve		40,400	155,000

Financial statements

Balance Sheet *as at 31 December, 1980*

Liabilities	£	Assets	£
Issued share capital of		Land and buildings	410,000
500,000 ordinary £1		Plant and machinery	600,000
shares	500,000	Stocks	235,000
Reserves	50,000	Sundry debtors	249,000
	550,000		
Long-term bank loan		Cash at bank	30,000
at 15% £500,000			
interest accrued			
£25,000	525,000		
Sundry creditors	285,000		
Provision for tax	130,000		
Provision for			
dividend	34,000		
	1,524,000		1,524,000

B. The annual published accounts at the end of December 1980 of A.B. Audio Vision Ltd., a public company operating a string of retail shops, read as follows:

Profit and Loss Account

	£000	£000	
Sales		300,000	
less:			
Opening stock	40,000		(It would
Purchases	220,000		be unusual
	260,000		for these
Closing stock	85,000		details to
Cost of goods sold	175,000		be pub-
			lished)
Wages and all other expenses	68,000		
Depreciation	3,000	246,000	
Trading profit		54,000	
Interest paid on debenture stock and			
bank lending		4,000	
Net profit before tax		50,000	
Corporation tax		26,000	
		24,000	
Dividends paid and recommended		15,000	
Reserved		9,000	

Balance sheet

	£000	£000	£000
Fixed assets			
Land and buildings		79,000	
Furniture and fittings		13,500	
Vehicles		2,000	94,500
Current assets			
Stock		85,000	
Debtors		24,000	
Bank		500	
		109,500	
Current liabilities			
Creditors (inc. tax)	38,000		
Dividend	10,000		
Bank loan	2,000	50,000	59,500
			154,000
Financed by:			
£1 ordinary shares issued		100,000	
Reserve		29,000	
		129,000	
Debenture stock		25,000	154,000

Calculate:
Current ratio
Liquid ratio
Quick ratio
Current assets turnover
Stock turnover
Working capital turnover
Mark-up
Gross profit ratio
Net return on capital employed
Net return on working capital
Net earnings per share (*see* Chapter 6)
Dividend cover
Net dividend per share (state gross equivalent, assuming 30% tax rate)
Gross dividend yield on ordinary shares priced at 180p.
Prices/Earnings ratio (state whether gross or net) at a price of 180p.

Appendix

Social security benefits

Under the United Kingdom social security scheme, payments made to individuals in cash (as distinguished from services such as medical, educational, dental, etc.) are called 'benefits'. There are three general classes of benefit:

(a)　those that can be paid only if the required national insurance contributions have been paid (national insurance benefits);

(b)　those that all persons who fulfil the required conditions are entitled to receive, irrespective of national insurance contributions and irrespective of what other means they may have (non-contributory benefits);

(c)　those that are dependent on what other money the claimant has coming in and which are not dependent on national insurance contributions (means-tested benefits)

The main benefits are listed in the following table, grouped not according to class but according to the circumstances in which they may be claimed. The list is not exhaustive; benefits likely to be of interest to only a small minority (*e.g.* Guardian's Allowance) have been omitted. To obtain a more precise account of all benefits available you should refer in the first instance to leaflet FB 2 (*Which Benefit? 60 Ways to get Cash Help*) and to the leaflet NP 12 (*Social Security : School-leavers and Students*), available from the local social security office or from the Department of Health and Social Security at Alexander Fleming House, Elephant and Castle, London SE1.

Appendix

In the second column of the table the following abbreviations have been used to indicate the class of benefit:

NI = national insurance benefit;
NC = non-contributory benefit;
MT = means-tested benefit.

The weekly amounts for each benefit quoted in the table are those applying from November 1980. An additional blank column has been provided to enable a reader to insert, after November 1981, the then current figures from an up-to-date copy of leaflet NI 196 *Social Security Benefit Rates* obtainable from the local social security office or from the Department of Health and Social Security.

Benefit	Type	Qualifying Conditions	Weekly amount	
			from Nov. 1980	*from Nov. 1981*
Dependent children				
Child benefit	NC	Responsibility for each child aged under 16 (or under 19 if receiving full-time education)	£4.75 per child	
Extra child benefit	NI or NC	As above but claimant in receipt of national insurance retirement or invalidity benefit	£7.50	
		As above, but in receipt of unemployment, sickness or maternity allowance.	£1.25	
Child benefit increase	NC	First or only child of certain lone persons	£3.00	
Child's special allowance	NI	Divorced woman with a child or children	£7.50 per child	

Benefit	Type	Qualifying Conditions	Weekly amount from Nov. 1980	from Nov. 1981
Illness				
Sickness benefit	NI	Prevention by incapacity from following normal employment	£20.65 plus earnings-related supplement. Extra £12.75 for wife or other dependent adult plus £1.25 for each dependent child. Payable for 28 weeks of sickness	
Invalidity pension (i)	NI	Incapacity extending beyond 28 weeks during which sickness benefit has been paid.	£26.00 plus £15.60 for wife plus £7.50 for each child	
		Additional allowance where incapacity occurs:		
		before age 40	£5.45	
		before age 50	£3.45	
		before age 60 (55 if a woman)	£1.75	

Invalidity pension (ii)	NC	Incapacity extending beyond 196 days of those whose NI contributions fail to qualify them for invalidity pension (i)	£16.30 plus £9.80 for wife plus £7.50 for each child
Industrial injury Industrial injury benefit	NC	Incapacity for work as the result either of an industrial accident or of certain prescribed diseases	£23.40 (£20.65 if aged 16 and under 18 with no entitlement to dependency benefit), plus £12.75 for wife and £1.25 per child. Payable for maximum of 26 weeks from date of accident or development of disease.
Industrial disability benefit	NC	Disability due to accident or disease remaining after 26 weeks of disability. Benefit normally commences on cessation of industrial injury benefit	Depends on severity of disablement. See leaflets NI 2, 3, 6, & 207

Benefit	*Type*	*Qualifying Conditions*	*Weekly amount* from Nov. 1980	*from Nov. 1981*
Industrial death benefit	NC	Death due to accident or disease resulting from work. Payable to widow or other dependant.	£38.00 for 26 weeks plus earnings-related supplement, followed by £27.70 or £8.15 depending on circumstances. Additions for dependent children	
Out of work Unemployment benefit	NI	Inability of person normally employed to obtain employment, but see leaflet NI 12	Basic rate of £20.65 plus £12.75 for wife and £1.25 for each child. Also earnings-related supplement. Payable for maximum period of 1 year	

(Note: Those out of work but whose NI contributions are insufficient to qualify them for this benefit (*e.g.* school-leavers) may claim supplementary benefit (see below)

Earnings-related supplement	NI or NC	Additional increment to sickness, unemployment benefit and some other benefits	Depends on actual earnings. This benefit is being phased out and will cease from 3 January 1982	

Redundancy payments	NC	Those made redundant after two years continuously with one employer	Tax-free lump sum in respect of each year of service with the employer of from ½ week's to 1½ week's pay per year of service, according to age. Only 20 years can count, and £110 is the maximum weekly wage to count
TOPS training allowance	NC	People who, after the lapse of 3 years following cessation of full-time education after age 16, take a training course under the Training Opportunities Scheme of the Manpower Services Commission	For the duration of the course: living at home £27.55; living away from home £24.05, plus reasonable cost of board and lodging. Also some earnings-related increase plus £9.75 for dependent spouse plus an allowance for each child
Employment rehabilitation allowance	NC	People aged over 20 who are undertaking a rehabilitation course to enable them to resume work after illness	As for TOPS above

Benefit	*Type*	*Qualifying Conditions*	*Weekly amount* *from Nov. 1980*	*from Nov. 1981*
Income not enough to live on				
Family income supplement	MT	People bringing up children on a low wage from full-time work. (See leaflet FIS 1)	Depends on family income and number of children. *e.g.* 2 children and income below £37.19, £18.50 benefit; or on income of £73.79, 20p benefit	
Supplementary benefit	MT	People over 16 and not working full-time. Can be paid on top of other benefits or earnings from part-time work. Unemployed school-leavers may claim this benefit, as may any unemployed person on cessation of unemployment benefit after 12 months. People with savings over £2,000 do not qualify.	According to his circumstances a person is deemed to have a weekly 'requirement' of income. If a person's income from all sources is below this 'requirement' level the difference is paid to him as a benefit **Example 1:** Requirement of single person aged 16–17 living at home is £13.10 plus £2.15 rent; over age 18 the requirement is £17.05 plus £2.15	

(For further details see leaflet SB 9)

Example 2: Requirement of a tenant householder is £21.30 plus actual rent if reasonable less deductions for non-allowable items

Example 3: Requirement of single person living in lodgings is the reasonable cost of board and lodging plus £7.10 personal expenses

Example 4: Requirement of a married couple is £34.60 plus from £7.30 to £17.05 per dependent child according to age. Husband also receives (if a tenant) the amount of his rent and rates, or (if owner) mortgage interest, rates and £65 per year towards repairs, etc.

Benefit	*Type*	*Qualifying Conditions*	*Weekly amount* *from Nov. 1980*	*from Nov. 1981*
Rent and rates rebate	MT	People who have difficulty in finding the money to pay rent and rates and are not receiving supplementary benefit	**Example:** Couple with two children and income of £70 a week and who pay £10 a week rent would get £4.68 benefit for rent. They may also qualify for a rates rebate	
Expecting a baby Maternity allowance	NI	Expectant mother who fulfils NI contribution conditions in her own right	£20.65 up to 18 weeks plus earnings-related supplement plus £1.25 for any dependent child	
Maternity grant (will be non-contributory from 1982)	NI	Mother or mother-to-be, claimable from 14 weeks before expected birth or up to 3 months after birth, on her own or husband's contributions	A single payment of £25 for each baby that lives more than 12 hours, but if all die one grant will be paid	

School and college

Educational maintenance allowance (also uniform and clothing grants)	MT	Parents who keep a child at school after age 16 and have not much money coming in	Depends on circumstances; refer to Education Welfare Officer
Students' grants and allowances	MT	Students on full-time further education courses including first degree or similar and teacher training	Basic allowance of £1,245 per year outside London, but depends on circumstances

Handicapped or disabled

Attendance allowance	NC	People who are severely disabled, physically or mentally, and who have needed a lot of looking after for over 6 months	£14.45 for day *or* night attendance; £21.65 for day *and* night attendance
Invalid care allowance	NC	Men or single women under pension age who cannot work because of the need to be at home to attend a severely disabled relative who is receiving attendance allowance	£16.30 plus £9.80 for wife or other adult dependant plus £7.50 for each child

Benefit	*Type*	*Qualifying Conditions*	*Weekly amount* from Nov. 1980	from Nov. 1981
Mobility allowance	NC	Those over 5 and under 65 unable or virtually unable to walk through disability and likely to remain so for at least 1 year	£14.50	
Retirement Retirement pension		(See Chapter 2 for full details)	Basic single person £27.15; married couple £43.45	
Widows Widow's allowance	NI	Widows other than those over 60 whose husbands were retirement pensioners.	£38 plus £7.50 for each child plus earnings-related supplement. Paid for first 26 weeks of widowhood	

Widowed mother's allowance	NI	Widow of any age with at least one qualifying child under 19. Payable on cessation of Widow's Allowance (see above)	£27.15 plus £7.50 for each child.
Widow's pension	NI	Widows over 40 who, having no dependent children do not qualify for widowed mother's allowance	From £8.15 to £27.15
Death grant	NI	Next of kin of deceased	£9 to £30 dependent on age of deceased.

(Benefit rates change each November. For up-to-date rates refer to current issue of leaflet NI 196)

Some additional reading and teaching aids

Chapter

1 *Pay Systems* by R.H.S. Beauchamp, Heinemann, 1979.
 Leaflets, notably 'National Insurance contributions for employees', available from local Social Security offices.

2 'Retirement pension' (leaflet NI 15), available from local Social Security offices.
 'The new state pension', an audio-visual programme available free from the Central Office of Information or from the Department of Health and Social Security, Alexander Fleming House, Elephant and Castle, London SE1.
 Set of six booklets on company pensions, free from The Company Pensions Information Centre, 7 Old Park Lane, London W1.
 'Pension rights on changing jobs', available free from the Occupational Pensions Board, Apex Tower, High Street, New Malden, Surrey.

3 'Paying tax for the first time', leaflet available free from your local tax office, or from the Inspector of Taxes.
 Hambro Tax Guide, Macdonald and Jane's, available annually in the autumn.

4 'Taxation and the building society investor', available free from The Building Societies Association, 34 Park Street, London W1Y 3PF.
 'Investing and saving into the 80s', *Money Which?,* June 1979.
 'Building societies survey', *Planned Savings,* June 1979.
 Free leaflets from banks, building societies, post offices and the National Savings Committee.

5 *A Guide to Savings and Investment* by James Rowlett, Pan, 1979.
 Theory and Practice of Investment by T.G. Goff, Heinemann, 3rd edn, 1980.
 'Government stock on the National Savings Register', available free from the National Savings Committee or any post office.

6 *A Guide to Savings and Investment* by James Rowlett, Pan, 1979.

Chapter

(6) *Theory and Practice of Investment* by T.G. Goff, Heinemann, 3rd edn, 1980.

Success in Investment by P.S. Roots, John Murray, 1974.

'The Stock Exchange – how it works'; 'A company – how it is financed'; 'The Stock Exchange'; 'How does The Stock Exchange Work?'; 'The settlement of business'; 'Why have a Stock Exchange?'. All these leaflets are available free from the Public Relations Department, The Stock Exchange, Old Broad Street, London EC2N 1HP.

7 Leaflets from multiple stores, finance companies and banks.

8 *Buying a House or Flat* by L.E. Vickers, Penguin, 1977 (new edn. due 1981).

'Building societies and house purchase'; 'Hints for home buyers'; 'Taxation and the building society borrower'. All these leaflets are available free from the Building Societies Association, 34 Park Street, London W1.

'Mortgages', *Money Which?*, December 1977.

'New homes', *Money Which?*, March 1978.

'Low-cost endowment mortgages', *Planned Savings,* February 1979.

11 *Hambro Tax Guide,* Macdonald and Jane's, available annually in the autumn.

12 *How to Plan your Life Insurance* by Christopher Gilchrist, Woodhead-Faulkner, 1979.

'House buildings insurance', *Money Which?*, June 1978.

Set of seven leaflets on general insurance and a booklet 'About insurance' (not available at time of going to press), all available from The British Insurance Association, Aldermary House, Queen Street, London EC4N 1TU.

'What is life assurance?' and 'Teachers' guide to life assurance', both available free from The Life Offices Association, Aldermary House, Queen Street, London EC4N 1TP.

13, *Management Accounting* by W.M. Harper, Macdonald & Evans, 2nd
14 edn, 1977.

Understanding Company Financial Statements by R.H. Parker, Penguin, 1972.

Interpreting Company Reports and Accounts by Geoffrey Holmes and Alan Sugden, Woodhead-Faulkner, 1979 (new edn due 1981).

Students may be encouraged to keep up-to-date by regularly reading the financial pages of the Saturday editions of *The Times, Guardian, Daily Telegraph* and *Daily Express,* the *Daily Mail's* 'Moneymail' feature on Wednesdays, the Monday issue of the *Financial Times* for prices and yields, and the business sections of the *Sunday Times, Observer* and *Sunday Telegraph.* A growing number of television and radio programmes deal with money matters that are sometimes relevant to the Personal and Business Finance examination syllabus and particularly appropriate is *The Money Programme* on BBC television.

Index